CW00747291

ISBN 978-0-578-70723-5

First cover image and other illustrations in the book are products of the author's imagination, inspired by ancient texts.

First published edition 2020

Author Email address: M.A.Quraani@outlook.com

Contents

Introduction

When I first started my journey in searching for truth, I knew my chances are limited, and this journey may drain my whole life before I arrive at a solid conclusion. However. Hope and stubbornness kept me going. I don't know if I should feel fortunate or not, because it led me to the true meaning of our inevitable destiny, death.

The ability to confront the truth requires a lot of courage, whether we believe in truth or not. Confronting our axioms and legacies is not a simple job even for the most intelligent people. Once we decide to walk through this path, there is no way back. We may end up uncertain and skeptical, or we could be lucky enough to find the answers that we are looking for. No matter how small or big the question is, without luck -bless- most likely we will not reach our aim.

In this book, I will share my journey to pursue the answers to the great spiritual questions. *Is there an afterlife? Does God exist? Do the ancient holy books have any truth in them? Will I be judged for my deeds?* If my journey was to be fruitful, I realized that I couldn't rely on faith alone – I had to have a convincing evidence. In this book, I will demonstrate the meaning behind the belief of an afterlife and the belief of God. Here, I work at the intersection of science and religion. I employ scientific researches and philosophical argument to study some of the most radical claims of scripture – and to reinterpret some of mankind's most dearly held beliefs.

I trust human intellect to choose the right answers and I believe every human being is an earnest seeker of truth despite his/her background or system of beliefs.

If you want to know the true meaning of life, death, and the afterlife, in this book, you will find a coherent rational meaning that most likely you haven't heard it before -I seem to be very confident, if you wait till the end of the book you may understand why I feel so.

I worked hard to summarize the book and make it as simple as possible, so you can read and comprehend the whole idea of the book. I recommend you complete the 10 chapters because it may have the answers to questions that come up in your mind while you are reading the book.

PART ONE : THE CLEANSING

Chapter 1

A Godless Afterlife

I have never seen the slightest scientific proof of the religious idea of heaven and hell, of future life for individuals, or of a personal God.

-Thomas Edison

Death, and the mystery that follows, has haunted human beings ever since their thought process developed the complexity to ponder the consequences of such irreversible and draconian finality. Human consciousness is blessed with the capacity to comprehend the process by which it will cease to exist and cursed with the audacious stubbornness not to settle for such comprehension. Like most natural systems, human consciousness exists in a constant struggle against its eternal extinction. The difference is, as far as we understand, human consciousness is the only entity capable to both comprehend and imagine the existential horror of such oblivion.

To begin to comprehend death, we must reconcile a relatively effective solution mankind developed to wage war against the vanquisher of his dreams of immortality. This is the afterlife: a continuation of life, if on different terms, and perhaps following different ground rules of existence. As such, the afterlife has moved from its portrayal in the ancient sacred texts and myths, to its bastardization in popular culture and the common imagination. To understand this human mystery at its deepest level, we must return to the original sources.

One of the grandest accomplishments of humans, in historical terms, is the relationship developed with natural forces they could not fully comprehend. The other is a basic understanding of entities whose existence and motivations they could barely grasp, such as supernatural beings. These beings, many asserts, were nothing more than a consummation of all their greatest fears and aspirations. Faith in a personal God, in whose universe, and under whose laws human consciousness would continue to exist after the death of the body, has become the foundation of history's greatest religions. This faith has persisted as mankind's most powerful tool to combat the dreaded notion of eternal oblivion.[1]

Evidence of such beliefs are based on nothing more than delusions or "wish-fulfillments." Sigmund Freud referred to these as "religious instincts." According to Freud in his *Totem and Taboo*, such a mythology was developed so we did not have to deal with the fact that one day we all cease to exist in our current state.[2] After all, this is the only state we know, or of which we have any memory. Perhaps there is a deeper and nobler truth hidden in the mystery of faith and the relationship with a superior entity. If allowed to persist

---

[1] L. T. Zagzebski. 1991. *The Dilemma of Freedom and Foreknowledge* (New York: Oxford University Press).
[2] Sigmund Freud. 1950. *Totem and Taboo* (New York: W. W. Norton and Company), 87.

rather than being impulsively and reductively dismissed as the stuff of fairy tales, might it shed light on that undiscovered place from which no traveler has fully returned?

Next, I would like to introduce my methodology for creating a better grasp on this topic. First, I must construct a framework by which I can select the necessary historical material to assist in my personal investigation of death and the afterlife. Much of this material includes passages from the sacred texts that, in ancient times, dealt with the mystery of death more unflinchingly than any other. I can then evaluate such material in as evenhanded, sober, and unbiased a manner as possible.

A search for the truth must be as unflinching, as it accepts various traditions and perspectives. This search will primarily rely on analyses and contextualization of religious texts, scientific investigations, and data. It will also call on the work of philosophers and artists—not as proof, but to lend meaning. Philosophers and artists' work also helps demonstrate the intensity of human beings' perennial gestures to grasp the ungraspable, such as eternal life. Afterward, I will move on from these texts into the modern religion and mythmaking of science. Only recently have these topics been given serious consideration regarding what may exist beyond the purlieus of our understanding of human consciousness.

Of course, no thinker, no matter how conscientious and vigilant, can ever claim to be truly unbiased. We are intellectual creatures shaped by our cultures. Growing up surrounded by all kinds of conflicts—political, cultural, and religious—I developed into someone well aware of the dangers of biases and prejudices. In this investigation I have made a commitment to look for the truth, no matter where it may lie, and follow it to wherever it leads. I also cast my net widely, not only to include a variety of sacred texts, but to employ different disciplines and methods.

To begin this cleansing of personal biases and purging of cultural prejudices, I have purposefully begun my search by putting monotheistic cultural and religious foundations to the test. Such religions, while not always central to mankind's existence, have in the past two millennia come to dominate religious philosophy, thought, and discussion.

My main questions, in this first part of the hunt for the truth, can be stated as follows:

Does a personal God exist?

Do the portrayals and promises of an afterlife in the ancient texts express unique universal truths?

How are such truths connected to the existence of a personal God?

Are the fantastic aspects of narratives that mirror the portrayal of life after death—such as the creation myths—just fairy tales, or do they have as much to teach us about the end of days as they do about our origins? This investigation delves into the connection between these two major events—the beginning and the end of time, the creation and destruction of the universe of man—in search for clues about what may lie beyond.

According to the Oxford English Dictionary, the word "God" for Christianity and other monotheistic religions means, "the creator and ruler of the universe and source of all moral authority; the supreme being." This type of entity is only conceived of as real and active in history in the ancient sacred books. The only source for this kind of God exists in ancient texts. It comes from the people who claimed to be prophets or messengers of this supreme being. The evidence I am looking for should come from these books, and it has to follow some of the criteria which follows.

In order to be intellectually true, the evidence need not be reductive. It should be objective, acceptable, and comprehensible to any thinker, regardless of cultural or religious beliefs. For the evidence to be deemed scientific, it should be based on accepted scientific foundations and consensus or come from accredited studies.

For me to be convinced the ancient books had a Godly source, the evidence should come from within the sacred books rather than other sources. Thus, the analysis here will involve a close look at the text. Any discussions of deviations from previous interpretation will remain confined to its resonance or echo in other sacred texts and not its history of scholarly interpretation.

Before exploring the subject of death and afterlife, I had to go through some other religious beliefs, like creationism, historical events, miracles, and morality. As follow is my opinion in these subjects.

The Beginning of Existence

The stories of the creation of the universe and beginning of life bear some textual and structural relation to the more eschatological texts that we will be considering. They both address periods in human time, outside of the realm of recorded history: the first because written language was not yet in use, and the second because it has not yet occurred, thus it is "beyond" the historical as we understand it. Therefore, it is somewhat ironic that, to shed light on both these "events" and seek to come to a greater understanding of the phenomenon of death, we must use as a tool, human language, which is limited in its capability to express existence outside of the temporal.

There is no bigger debate between theist and atheist thinkers than the one dealing with the nature of the creation of our world; how we interpret the forces at work in it, and clues to offer to our origins. Thus, I will give equal weight to the holy texts and scientific theories, such as the big bang and the multiverse theories that explain how our universe came into existence. Other theories that address the development of life through change and transformation, such as evolution, can be studied as game changers in perspective, using strategies we may employ in an attempt to come to a fuller understanding of the afterlife.

More complex theories of origin, such as intelligent design, which insists the very complexity and symmetry of the universe bears the signature of its designer, are more in keeping with modern science. Yet, the proofs of a Godhead as first mover, however general such an entity may be, does not directly address the role of a personal God in the mystery of death and a personal afterlife.

Thus, we run into our first philosophical and rhetorical quandary.

How depersonalized can a personal God become before such an entity is considered a natural force? A corollary to this question, tailored to address our concerns, vis-à-vis death and the afterlife, specifically concerns human consciousness; that is, how depersonalized can a human consciousness become before it is not considered an individual or personal consciousness anymore? When is it a spiritual presence, a metaphysical aura, a memory, or a ghost? All are formidable forces, but not something fairly defined as an individual conscience.

For instance, Carl Jung theorized there is a collective human unconscious that exists in perpetuity with the species accumulating memory, culture, and such.[3] This "consciousness" is contained both in humans individually and as a group, existing with us in our lifetimes and beyond us, changed ever so infinitesimally by the

---

[3] C. G. Jung. 1953. *Collected Works,* Volume 7 (Princeton, NJ: Princeton University Press), 437–507.

individual experience of every human who has ever lived. But this is not the eternity we are after.

The End of Days and the Afterlife

Most of these religious texts are concerned with the history of human beings living a life of engagement with others and with their Gods. They are concerned with how such creatures may best benefit each other and the world they live in; many narratives present the afterlife as the culmination of a life fully experienced in our world. That is, the End of Days is pretty meaningless as a concept, without taking into account the parade of days that led to such an end.

Thus, I will take a three-pronged approach in dissecting this philosophy from the holy texts, both from material in the texts and from analyses by the scholars who followed. This approach will focus on historical context, the intersection between the "miracle" of faith and reason, and the consequent moral authority assumed from such knowledge, as well as its relevance to belief in an afterlife.

Historical Events

Did the great flood really happen? Did people from history such as Jesus, Krishna, or Gautama Buddha really exist? These are hotly debated subjects between religion and science, which is the truth or existence of the historical characters and the events, and natural phenomena that are portrayed in the ancient books. One of the basic functions of these books, no doubt, was to record the history of the specific culture from which they arose. Often the research or the science do not unearth the necessary evidence to prove beyond doubt that the events or characters existed, as portrayed in the books.

Such conclusions are reached coldly and with a lack of nuance or analytic versatility in that they often are performed too retroactively from our vantage point. These evaluations neglect such things as the value of fable and myth in portraying truth. In these more primitive human narratives, there was little distinction between fictional and nonfictional narratives. What we now consider techniques and tools from both genres were used. The truth may have been defined more loosely in cultures in which the knowledge of the natural world was less precise, and speculations about it, more mystical and connected to mythical stories. Historical knowledge tended to be retained within the confines of myth.

Faith as a Miracle

Many religious people believe in miracles that have been mentioned in the ancient books, but for me, that on its own has never been enough to make me a believer. Even if miracles really occurred as described, such phenomena, if witnessed and confirmed, provide only proof and revelation for the people present. Such secondhand testimony is not enough proof for me, perhaps because such accounts can be exploited for motivations that have little to do with the truth. If such events happened in our time, they could have been subject to scientific explanations.

Is faith its own miracle and therefore proof unto itself? The miracles in this case are not so much a disruption of the natural order that they could motivate us to question it, but more to the matter, a manifestation of the very act of faith, which must reach beyond the frontier. The miracles are thus a manifestation of faith and not some sleight of hand intended to dupe.

Morality

In ancient times, when people had limited resources for survival, they had to be offered kind of encouragement. They needed a system of rewards and punishments for their deeds. Things were iffy and unstable in the morning hunt and during the harsh winters. Early humans thought it best to establish a moral code in which acts such as killing your cave mate, stealing his dinner, or planting your seed in his sexual partner would be harshly punished. Like any other aspect of human life, ethics and morality are progressive in relation to human development. How has such a progression affected our moral authority in current times? Do human beings still need a God and the dogma that supports such an entity to dictate moral behavior?

After reviewing evidence from a wide variety of traditions and cultures, I couldn't find any definitive evidence that would lead me to believe in a personal God. I also did not consider my status as an unbeliever in conflict with those with faith. Neither did I fly a banner and invade the opposing camps with assaults on their intelligence or patronizing put-downs about their anachronistic spiritual evolution.

My search had neither been a success or a failure. At the least, its success should not be judged by its conclusions. Success, I decided, was best determined by the sincerity and openness in which I pursued the questions that arose. My loss on a personal level came after the initial investigations of my search. Sadly, I had relinquished, along with a belief in God, belief in the possibility of eternal life.

Or so it seemed.

Monotheistic texts are almost wholly consistent when it comes to the inseparable nature of the promise of eternal life and the eternal Godhead that presides over such a world. The chosen ones must prove their mettle in this world and often commit themselves entirely to the Godhead before the paradise of eternal life is achieved. To continue my investigation into what happens after death, and whether we continue to exist as beings even if in a different form, I had to abandon some of my cultural biases. While the concept of an afterlife without a Godhead presiding over it at first seemed as attractive as sitting through a slasher movie marathon, I had to purposefully readjust my focus. What I did was to imagine the separation of the Godhead from the idea of eternal life.

The next question was, what would be our guide and benchmark to delineate the progress of how we pass from one stage to another on the frontiers of death? The conceit of an engaged and committed life as a pathway is a phenomenon that is still very much with us. It may shed more light on the subject of earthly life and its relation to the afterlife, which starts by death.

Chapter 2

The Biggest Deception

Let us follow the truth whither so ever it leads.

-Socrates

Before I began my investigating into the phenomena of death, to study the proofs for an afterlife, I had to go through major stories believers use to confirm their faith. If a story has a new and credible interpretation, it will demolish the argument of the believers.

An old but treasured and sacred story is often best served when understood in perhaps an extremely new way. What happens when we search for a new way to interpret an old story? Are there wrong ways to understand stories, which for centuries have been imagined in a singular way by believers convinced that to dare to look at it from any other perspective would seem like sacrilege?

Can we invalidate the truth in a holy narrative by daring to look at it with fresh eyes?

Or do we enrich its truth?

Do we lend it new power?

One of the most iconic stories in Western culture is one that seems to insist on a limited range of interpretations.

According to the New Testament and the words of Jesus Christ, he was resurrected after being crucified.[4] This is perhaps the best-known story of resurrection, though it is far from the only example, and not even close to the earliest narrative with such a plot. Examples abound, such as the Egyptian God Osiris being cut into pieces and reassembled whole,[5] and the warrior Achilles, stolen from his funeral pyre by his mother and brought back to life as a God.[6] In Western culture, however, only the resurrection of Lazarus, for which Christ was responsible, rivals this story in infamy.[7]

So, what does the physical resurrection of Christ prove to believers? Does it prove the existence of a personal God?

Scientifically, this story cannot be accepted as truth for a wide variety of reasons. An important reason is that there has never been proof of the resurrection of any human being. Still, the followers of the Christian Church, many of whom can be counted as respected scientists, have believed this story for centuries and have accepted it as a central and essential tenet of their faith.

In this chapter, I examine this story using the three-pronged approach established in the first chapter, but inverting the order to deal with the miracle on which the faith is based first. Next, I will establish its historical context. Finally, we return to the New

---

[4] Matthew 28:1–10 (New International Version).
[5] J. Gwyn *Griffiths. 1960. The Conflict of Horus and Seth (Liverpool, England: Liverpool University Press).*
[6] Proclus, Chrestomathia ii.
[7] John 11:41–44.

Testament and examine Christ's words about false disciples. It is upon this discussion that we base a conclusion.

The Miracle

The Godhead does not entirely prove the resurrection, not directly. It does offer Christians a promise that implies a world that includes the culmination of the promise of the Trinity: "If the Spirit of him who raised Jesus from the dead dwells in you, he who raised Christ Jesus from the dead will give life to your mortal bodies also through his Spirit who dwells in you."[8] It is in the promise of the Holy Spirit dwelling within Jesus that makes the promise of the Trinity, and thus of God, become one with the resurrection in traditional Christian belief.

This, in turn, is connected with the central verse in Christian belief: the campaign slogan of sorts. And if you don't buy into this slogan, you cannot be part of the party or the good news that it brings: "For God so loved the world, that He gave his only begotten Son, that whosoever believeth in him should not perish, but have everlasting life."[9]

The implication is that those who do not believe, will perish, and will not have everlasting life. They will not be resurrected. You have to do some semantic contortions to interpret this important verse any other way. But just in case, Catholic thinkers, such as

---

[8] Romans 8:10.
[9] John 3:16.

Thomas Aquinas, have taken this a step further. They used this verse not only as a testament of the deity in Christ, but as a clever rhetorical way to entwine the truth, the resurrection and the truth of the Trinity. As Aquinas writes in a commentary on this verse: "Since the Father is true God, and Christ is true God, it follows that the true God sent the true God."[10]

For other thinkers, such as Augustine, this love for the God as incarnate flesh, the Christ made truth in the sacrifice of crucifixion, is the highest form of love. This is what God grants to believers, and that can only be redeemed in the resurrection. This type of love is impossible without redemption.

The miracle of the resurrection in traditional Christian belief is not an isolated event, nor is it a replication of other resurrections, such as that of Lazarus (or Osiris and Achilles). It is part of a sacred chain of phenomena on which belief rests. It proves not only God's existence but the existence of an afterlife, promised by belief. The two can no more be separated than the Trinity can be broken into separate and independent parts.

What if we attempt such a separation, doing so not from external forces, but from within? The following sections begin to offer a new perspective on this act. It uses not only passages in the Gospels but perspectives on the life of Jesus from believers.

---

[10] St. Thomas Aquinas. "Commentary on the Gospel of St. John." Translated by James A. Weisheipl (Albany, NY: Magi Books, Inc.), 540.

Historical Jesus

Various interpretations of the historical Jesus intersect. Sometimes, conflict arises with the religious interpretation of the Godhead. Believers and thinkers, such as John Dominic Crossan, Albert Schweitzer, and others, offer such perspectives. Often, however, because there is such a scarcity of primary sources on the life of Christ, such investigations rely more on conjecture, speculation, and outright educated guesses. Speculative work is not necessarily the type of "history" that can be trusted to yield facts. Thus, the character created by the Gospelists is the one that remains at the center of human perception.

Regardless, this has not prevented writers from envisioning Jesus in various primary roles. He has been called prophet in the rabbinical tradition, philosopher, political revolutionary, eschatological thinker, and a myth. In various of these guises, Crossan has argued, Jesus serves more to advance the philosophical, theological, or political agenda of the writer at hand, than anything else. These guises represent a banner Jesus, more than a historical character.[11]

Thus, for the historical Jesus to serve any purpose in this investigation, it is necessary to get closer to the source and not just to his words. We need access to encounters, as well as the writings of his disciples and other followers, such as Paul of Tarsus. Belief,

---

[11] John Dominic Crossan. 2009. *Jesus: A Revolutionary Biography* (New York: HarperOne).

not just on the life and death of Jesus, but also on the effect and interpretation of his resurrection and its consequences, can best be culled from his followers.

No doubt, among Jesus's contemporaries, Paul stands tall. He is among those responsible for spreading the word not only of Christ's teachings, but also the importance of the resurrection. The resurrection is the promise both Aquinas and Augustine later interpreted as the highest truth and highest love.

Throughout the ages, Christians have relied on Paul's perception of the resurrected Christ, a perception that traditionally holds to this day. The triumph over death through the resurrection, according to Paul in his First Letter to the Corinthians, is the starting point of the ultimate victory over death for all believers in a state: "Thus it is written, 'The first man Adam became a living being'; the last Adam became a life-giving spirit. But it is not the spiritual which is first but the physical, and then the spiritual."[12] This leads us to suspect Christianity has been, more than anything, a Paulist religion historically.

But what about Christ's other contemporaries, his disciples who were with him throughout his ministry?

> Now Thomas, one of the twelve, called the Twin, was not with them when Jesus came. So, the other disciples told him, "We have seen the Lord." But

---

[12] 1 Corinthians 15:44–46.

he said to them, "Unless I see in his hands the
mark of the nails and place my finger into the
mark of the nails, and place my hand into his side,
I will never believe."[13]

That's someone who seems to be more in the spirit of our
investigation. Although Thomas's doubts have been iconized not
only as a failure of imagination but a failure of the very instinct of
faith, he was not the only one who reacted in such a manner. In all
different sources of this story, you can notice something in common,
which is the disbelief of the disciples. Notice, for example, the
"startled and frightened" disciples in Luke 24, to whom Christ again
has to prove that it's him by almost comically pointing at his
wounds. "Why are you troubled, and why do doubts arise in your
hearts? See my hands and my feet, that it is I myself. Touch me and
see. For a spirit does not have flesh and bones as you see that I
have."[14]

This is very strange for people who lived with him for a long
period of time, and those specifically to whom the resurrection had
been foretold: "But after I have risen, I will go ahead of you into
Galilee."[15]

For individuals forewarned that they were going to be
witnesses to this great event—those who have believed so strongly

---

[13] John 20:24–25.
[14] Luke 24:38–40.
[15] Matthew 26:32

in their master that they have left behind homes, professions, and families to follow him—they sure act spooked and suspicious about the truth of the resurrection when the time comes. You would think that the way they have been prepared for it, they would either be searching for him or planning a huge celebration. Instead, they do almost the opposite: they are skeptical and unbelieving, even so surprised that you could say they are shocked.

Why?

It may be partly human nature, for they were living in a time when such executions as the one Christ suffered were common. Moreover, Christ was not the first to claim the power of returning to the living. While they were no doubt zealous believers in the words and teachings of Christ, all but one abandoned him after he was arrested and went into hiding. Even his most beloved disciple, who would one day become the head of the new sect, denied he even knew him when questioned directly after Christ's arrest.[16]

They were human and, as such, they were terrified. They were justifiably skeptical, no matter how devoted they were. As I struggled to understand the reasons behind this discrepancy, I found other possible answers written in the Gospels.

The Morality of the Resurrection

---

[16] John 18:15–27

Jesus's own warnings to his disciples of the coming of false Christs also have to be taken into account. Did he expect others to claim his moral authority and warn the disciples about it?

"Not everyone who says to me, 'Lord, Lord,' will enter the kingdom of heaven, but the one who does the will of my Father who is in heaven. On that day many will say to me, 'Lord, Lord, did we not prophesy in your name, and cast out demons in your name, and do many mighty works in your name?' And then will I declare to them, 'I never knew you; depart from me, you workers of lawlessness."[17]

Did the disciples have this warning in mind when they doubted those who took on the mantle of his authority through the resurrection? Was this what caused them to be wary of anyone claiming to be their master? The idea of the danger of the false prophets was rooted in the mind of the disciples even. They saw them as a deception and temptation of which they should be wary and frightened. In a later chapter in Matthew, Christ is even more specific in his warning:

> "Take heed that no man deceive you. For many
> shall come in my name, saying, I am Christ; and
> shall deceive many."[18]

---

[17] Matthew 7:21–23.
[18] Matthew 24:4–5.

Deception of such magnitude is the work of the Great Deceiver. Christ himself underwent temptations laced with such deceit after forty days of fasting in the desert. During that time Satan tried to tempt him away from his role in salvation by offering him dominion over the world.[19] Accepting such deception as truth means veering away from the cardinal virtues that are the bedrock of Christ's teachings.

Again, the claiming of such direct authority, as Satan claims in the desert, was also something Christ warned his disciples against. And they asked him, "Teacher, when will these things be, and what will be the sign when these things are about to take place?" And he said, "See that you are not led astray. For many will come in my name, saying, 'I am he!' and, 'The time is at hand!' Do not go after them."[20] How then are we to heed these warnings considering other passages I have quoted, where he foretells his immediate physical resurrection?

To examine this fully, we should take into account one of the most interesting interrogations of Jesus. The interrogation about his mission and his place in his world conducted by Pontius Pilate could shed light.

> Pilate then went back inside the palace, summoned
> Jesus and asked him, "Are you the king of the

---

[19] Matthew 4:1–11.
[20] Luke 21:7–8.

Jews?" "Is that your own idea," Jesus asked, "or did others talk to you about me?" "Am I a Jew?" Pilate replied. "Your own people and chief priests handed you over to me. What is it you have done?" Jesus said, "My kingdom is not of this world. If it were, my servants would fight to prevent my arrest by the Jewish leaders. But now my kingdom is from another place."[21]

If Jesus's kingdom was indeed from another place, why have there been so many legions of kings, warriors, and conquistadors intent on claiming it in their lives, beginning immediately after Jesus's death? Can such characters then be considered the fake Christs of whom Jesus warned? And is the person or persons that the disciples met at the beginning of this historical repetitive cycle the first of them?

Christ didn't warn his disciples after his resurrection. He didn't say, "I will be resurrected and establish a kingdom in this world, then don't believe anyone after me." It is very clear he expected someone—or many—to impersonate him, or at least to take on the authority of his life and mission and warned the disciples about it. He added, if these fake Christs were not good enough, and if they did not perform signs and wonders to lead astray even the elect (the disciples), they shouldn't believe them. Did an impostor

---

[21] John 18:33–36.

Christ deceive the disciples and the whole world in the difficult days after the crucifixion?

If the physical resurrection is not necessary in Jesus's world, if it in fact may be antithetical to his teachings, what does this say about the necessity of the belief in it, vis-à-vis the moral authority of his life and teachings? Are the teachings of Jesus delegitimized without a resurrection? Based on my understanding of the scriptures, the resurrection did not occur, but such an interpretation was taken on, as he predicted, to lend moral authority to a movement. In the coming chapters, I will consider this in light of the aspects of death and the afterlife in other cultures.

Chapter 3

Death in the Ancient Books

The deepest sin against the human mind is to believe things without evidence.

-Thomas Henry Huxley

What do scriptures and ancient books say about death and the afterlife? How can we use such material and knowledge to craft a shield against what Thomas Henry Huxley said was the deepest sin against the human mind, to believe things without evidence?[22] The ancient books describe death as a separation of the immaterial soul from the physical body. The body will remain in the ground, while the soul will be taken to another place. Based on a person's deeds, he or she will then be rewarded or punished. This is a very hard concept to accept without evidence, however its role in crafting the foundations of an advanced civilization is clear. This latter matter is not the concern of this investigation.

It is possible that people in ancient times were privy to some kind of miracle that led them to revelation and belief. For me to believe in this manner, I must have evidence. The required evidence

---

[22] Laird Wilcox and John George, editors. 1994. *Be Reasonable* (Buffalo, NY: Prometheus Books), 270.

must be tested, not just on the basis of the content of these scriptures, but how such "truths" hold up in the world beyond these texts. First, let's see what ancient books have said about this stage in the journey of the human spirit, as it moves from one stage to another.

Undoubtedly, in a metaphorical sense, the human spirit is an evolving entity, as it moves from one state to the other, according to the forces acting upon it and those forces it can generate from within in response. This symbolic journey is often taken as a basis for the explanation of the passage of the spirit from the realm of the living body, beyond it, in the ancient books. This search forces us to move beyond the symbolic, and into what is real or true. Thus, the exploration of these books will be based not only on the belief and rituals they inspired, but also on factual evidence for their claims. I will address a few questions regarding such evidence in some of the ancient books, which concern the meaning of death. I will explore the following:

How is the text historically relevant from both a societal and cultural viewpoint?

How does belief in these texts lead to a pattern of behavior in life?

How is morality connected to interpretations of death and the afterlife in various aspects of the texts?

Egyptian Book of the Dead

The Egyptian Book of the Dead is basically a collection of spells or incantations meant to assist the dead in their dangerous passage from our world into that of the Gods and eternity. As such, it is a tool bag for survival in the afterlife, accompanied by stories that lay out for the reader the landscape of the underworld, and the creatures that inhabit it, including itinerant Gods and devious demons. The Egyptian ancient text asserts the souls of the dead will be judged, and their hearts will be weighed against the feather of truth.[23] If a person's soul passes the test of such scales, he or she will enter the land of the God, otherwise he or she will be given to Ammit, a being who represents punishment.

No two versions of this ancient text are alike. There is no such thing as a canonical edition. It represents a journey through the difficulties and travails of the world beyond death. In so doing, it is a very evocative representation of the Egyptian belief system of the afterlife. The book's ultimate purpose is to serve as a code for human behavior in this life.

Part of this purpose seems to be dictated by having lived a life in accordance with the truth. For although the book is a sort of survival guide for the wilderness of the underworld, no spell is provided to fool the main Gods, "the Entourage who make men" and

---

[23] British Museum. 2011. *Journey through the Afterlife: Ancient Egyptian Book of the Dead*, 6.

constitute the tribunal responsible for the weighing of the hearts. This tribunal is more concerned with the life lived before the journey. It is also concerned with how the heart of the journeyperson remained true to the dictates of the truth. In fact, the main God in the tribunal, Toth, is known as the "keeper of the truth."

Thus, part of the weighing of the deceased one's heart is based on "righteous deeds in the Great Balance, and no sin,"[24] but also on the fact that the soul which is judged "did not go about with deceitful speech while he was on earth." The spells that make up the majority of the book can be considered a sort of misdirection or trickery. Survival of the journey that leads to the ultimate tribunal, it only considers the previous life and its relationship to the truth. This condemnation of the false person or impostor, when it comes to the Self of the dead, resonates with Christ's warning to his disciples about false prophets who may seek to distort his message and teachings.

The idea of a life judged in accordance to the truth becomes an important benchmark in how we may judge the understanding of these ancient texts, vis-à-vis cultural and moral perspectives. Thus, judgment is not necessarily based on individual deeds, but according to the general arc of a person's moral life toward a moral principle, on the truth. As we shall see, this is a recurring theme.

---

[24] John H. C. Pippy. 2011. *Egyptian Origin of the Book of Revelation* (Raleigh, NC: Lulu Enterprises, Inc.), 160.

Tibetan Book of the Dead

In the Tibetan Book of the Dead, it is written that the deceased soul will go through different stages, and finally it will face some sort of scale. For each good thing, a white stone is awarded; for each sin, a black stone. Then, the soul is punished, if the black stones outnumber the white ones. The soul can redeem deficiencies in this scale by meditation and prayers. The individual can become a Buddha.[25]

The soul's struggle is about moving from its "alienated" state to an enlightened state like the Buddha. This evolution may be considered a moving from a fraudulent, fractured, or unreal self, to a "self" more in tune and in keeping with the complex reality of existence. This principle is best expressed in the text, in passages like the following:

> When he looks into the mirror of evolution all
> your sins and virtues will distinctly appear therein.
> Your lies will not help. Yama will tie a rope
> around your neck and lead you away. He will cut
> off your head, pull out your heart, rip out your
> guts, lick your brains, and drink your blood. But
> since you cannot die . . . you revive again.[26]

---

[25] *Tibetan Book of the Dead.* 1975. (Boston, MA: Shambhala Publications, Inc.), 36–37.
[26] Ibid., 37.

The alienated or fraudulent body containing the soul that has not evolved is very graphically depicted here, as something to be discarded violently before it can be remade. This is a painful experience that, nevertheless, does not end the existence of the being. The question concerning our investigation is how such a being "revives" again and what dictates the terms and consequences of such a "revival?"

Here again is the presentation of different aspects or emanations of the self, at struggle against each other in the process of living or not living according to dictates of truth and virtue. Success or failure, in this struggle, determines the initial condition of the afterlife. Unlike in the Egyptian Book of the Dead, in the Tibetan Book of the Dead there is not just the possibility, but the demand, for evolution of the self into a truer emanation.

Holy Zend-Avesta

In the Zend-Avesta, the holy book of Zoroastrianism, an ancient Persian religion, it is written that a soul of the dead person will pass through the Chinwad bridge and, based on its deeds and "on the worldly gifts that they gave away," either proceed or remain without passing.[27] This idea of moving from the "un-cleansed" world of life to the "cleansed" world of the afterlife repeats the motif central in many of these books. Within them, the soul of the

---

[27] A. V. Williams Jackson. 1893. *Avesta Reader* (Stuttgart, Germany: W. Kohlhammer), 79.

deceased shifts from one stage to another, according to the actions and spiritual undertakings during its life. The difficulty in passing the bridge will vary according to the soul, and at the end of the bridge is the reward. The soul that does not pass the bridge will be dragged to hell. As for those that successfully move on to the more evolved state in the afterlife:

> Then comes the beautiful, well-shapen, strong and
> well-formed maid, with the dogs at her sides, one
> who can distinguish, who has many children,
> happy, and of high understanding. She makes the
> soul of the righteous one go up above the Hara-
> berezaiti; above the Chinwad bridge she places it
> in the presence of the heavenly Gods themselves.[28]

This distinguishing of the high state of moral understanding is similar to the evolution in the Tibetan Book of the Dead, and the truth sought in the Egyptian Book of the Dead. Whereas most of the sections of the Zend-Avesta consist of guides to ritual practice, one specific section is concerned with moral law. It includes spells to fight off the temptations of demons. This section is called Vendidad, and it is structured as moral dialogues between Zoroaster and one of his disciples.

---

[28] James Darmesteter, translator. 1895. *The Zend-Avesta*, second edition (Oxford, England: Clarendon Press), 98.

The important element in this section concerning our exploration is its concern with living a life of high understanding. Such understanding is achieved through a practice of the principles laid out in this "moral guide," which addresses issues such as hygiene, mourning for the dead, the nature of diseases, respect for the sacred, and a veneration for nature. The section also includes penance to be paid for violations of these principles, offering the possibility for the kind of evolution that is central in the Tibetan Book of the Dead. The ultimate objective is a kind of cleansing that will allow the spirit of the deceased to cross the Chinwad bridge into the land of eternity, its cleansed state unmistakable and untarnished: "As to the Godly man that has been cleansed, the wicked evil-doing Daevas tremble at the perfume of his soul after death, as doth a sheep on which a wolf is pouncing."[29]

Holy Bible

The Holy Bible also mentions the immaterial soul that lives after death: the good will stay in the presence of God, and the wicked will go to a place of darkness, Sheol.

> Like sheep they are appointed for Sheol; death
> shall be their shepherd, and the upright shall rule
> over them in the morning. Their form shall be
> consumed in Sheol, with no place to dwell.[30]

---

[29] Ibid., 108.
[30] Psalm 49:14.

In opposition to this, is the promise of paradise to the righteous, which is very distinctly promised not just to the doers of good deeds but also to those who allow their spirit to evolve toward a higher understanding of classic virtues such as justice and compassion. One of the most memorable examples is the forgiveness of sins granted to one of the thieves crucified alongside Jesus Christ, not for a life well lived, but because of achieving a state of higher understanding and belief through his suffering and punishment.

One of the criminals who were hanged railed at him, saying, "Are you not the Christ? Save yourself and us!" But the other rebuked him, saying, "Do you not fear God, since you are under the same sentence of condemnation? And we indeed justly, for we are receiving the due reward of our deeds; but this man has done nothing wrong." And he said, "Jesus, remember me when you come into your kingdom." And he said to him, "Truly, I say to you, today you will be with me in paradise."[31]

The Bible also talks about a physical resurrection at the end of time (the Day of Judgment), and this also is mentioned in both the Old and New Testaments.[32] Therefore, the soul will be joined with the body once again at the end of time: "And many of those who sleep in the dust of the earth shall awake, some to everlasting life,

---

[31] Luke 23:39–43.
[32] Ecclesiastes 11:9; Matthew 12:36.

and some to shame and everlasting contempt."[33] Or those chosen are taken with their physical bodies to the rapture:

> So, will be the coming of the Son of Man. Then
> two men will be in the field; one will be taken and
> one left. Two women will be grinding at the mill;
> one will be taken and one left. Therefore, stay
> awake, for you do not know on what day your
> Lord is coming.[34]

This call to awaken is reminiscent of the Buddhist call to higher understanding of a more complex reality.

Quran

Quran is the most recent of these sacred texts, and it claims to be the last revelation from God, but it is not so different from the Bible in that it mentions the life of the soul after death, and the paradise for the good: "And never think of those who have been killed in the cause of God as dead. Rather, they are alive with their Lord, receiving provision."[35] It also addresses that the wicked will go to hell: "...And if you could but see when the wrongdoers are in the overwhelming pangs of death while the angels extend their hands, [saying], 'Discharge your souls! Today you will be awarded the punishment of [extreme] humiliation for what you used to say

---

[33] Daniel 12:2.
[34] Matthew 24:39–42.
[35] Sura 3:169.

against Allah other than the truth and [that] you were, toward His verses, being arrogant.'"[36] And like in the Holy Bible, there is also the promise of a physical resurrection at the time of reckoning:

> That is because Allah is the Truth and because He gives life to the dead and because He is over all things competent. And [that they may know] that the Hour is coming – no doubt about it – and that Allah will resurrect those in the graves.[37]

The suggestion here is that the effort and ability to reside in the realm of truth is crucial to the passage into everlasting life. This rings a familiar note also present in other holy texts. From here, we can conclude various things from this brief selection of sacred writings in regard to belief, living a "good" and "evolved" life, and the afterlife.

Scholars of different religions, especially Buddhists and Hindus, based on verses and interpretations of their holy texts, believe in some form of reincarnation, that the deceased soul will be reborn to other forms of physical life, based on what the person had done in previous lives. I will be discussing more about the concept of reincarnation at chapter 9. However, such beliefs can perhaps help us look at the concept of the afterlife, and the evidence for it,

---

[36] Sura 6:93.
[37] Sura 22:6–7.

less as a static condition and more as part of a process with which we are engaged from the moment we are born.

For sure there are many other ancient books that I haven't mentioned here, but notably, most of these books express a belief in the continuing existence of the consciousness and an eternal life in hell or heaven, not just as an objective or a leap of faith, but as the conclusion of a complex process that involves both the actions of beings and the understanding that they hold in their hearts, which, as fallen creatures, is always developing into something greater than themselves. Therefore, from here on, this exploration takes on the task of searching for evidence of these widespread and very similar claims of an afterlife based on the good life; that is, a life that seeks toward something beyond itself, a life that is bent toward the expansion of its present existence.

Chapter 4

Science and the Unknowable

To understand the actual world as it is, not as we should wish it to be, is the beginning of wisdom.

-Bertrand Russell

In the next two chapters, I would like to move from the religious to the scientific arenas, in an effort to build the foundation of evidence as proof of an afterlife. In so doing, various aspects will be considered, including studies done on consciousness, out-of-body experiences (OBEs), and near-death experiences (NDEs), in an attempt to come to terms with the entity that we call "the self" or "the psyche," which some have termed "the human spirit" or "the soul." By presenting scientific evidence that such an entity exists outside the physical processes and chemical reactions in the body, the groundwork for proof of an afterlife can be established. Even though they will readily admit such consciousness is beyond the physical body, many scientists will immediately balk at the very idea that human consciousness can be discussed as something separate from the body.

Establishing the possibility of such the afterlife, using scientific methods rather than the more poetic, mythical, and metaphysical strategies of the ancient religious narratives, expands the reach of this investigation. We will move into the heretofore mysterious realm of those exploring the very moment when consciousness either ends or passes to another dimension. Discussions, analyses, and evaluations in these two chapters rely on the conclusions of scientific experiments, such as those performed on rats, and the observations and evaluations of medical personnel who treat individuals who have undergone NDEs. This evidence is yielded primarily by studying those who flatline after suffering cardiac arrest, when the brain is deprived of oxygen. At this crucial moment, those undergoing cardiac arrest will soon decease without the rapid intervention of cardiopulmonary resuscitation (CPR). At this liminal stage, many individuals report having NDEs.

These experiences are somewhat varied in type, but they often involve the sensation of exiting the body and floating. Sometimes there are reports of observing the medical personnel struggling to revive the body's functions. Other similarities in the reports of NDEs across cultures include passage through a dark tunnel into an expanse of bright light, tranquility, and encounters with loved ones or spiritual entities. Moreover, there is the sensation of proximity to a threshold that cannot be crossed. Of course, the experience, for those who recounted them, also involves the eventual return to their physical bodies.

Before reviewing the evidence and arguments presented by both sides in the lively debate that has arisen in this new incursion into the nature of consciousness, let's first set the groundwork by defining some crucial elements.

A brain has "flatlined" when the sensors used to measure the organ's electrical activity show a flat line, which demonstrates that brain activity has ceased. Upon flatlining, the brain of the person in question neither receives nor responds to any type of stimuli. It has stopped functioning. If the person's brain has flatlined and they still experience consciousness, separate from body function, then human consciousness itself may not be wholly reliant on the brain for existence.

Some proponents, such as Dr. Sam Parnia, warn that much more expansive and comprehensive studies should be conducted on both OBEs and NDEs, as they suggest the possibility that the brain is merely a vessel of human consciousness and not its sole originator.[38] Parnia is too careful as a scientist to claim this is undeniably true. He does not even build any substantial theoretical framing around it, likely because of the mostly anecdotal evidence concerning NDEs and OBEs. He simply insists we don't know, and we should investigate this phenomenon much more rigorously, with an open mind.[39]

The mere suggestion of such a game-changing possibility based on subjective experience, even of hundreds of cases in uncontrolled settings, sets many neurologists into a frenzy. They point to studies that have discovered significant levels of activity in

---

[38] Sam Parnia. 2013. *Erasing Death* (New York: HarperCollins), 273.
[39] Ibid., 278.

brains below the surface cortex, even when the brain was flatlined according to machines that may not be equipped to measure deeper brain activity. They also suggest the likelihood that the dreamlike scenarios of NDEs and OBEs are concocted by the brain just before it enters, or as it comes out of, its nonfunctional stage. Other destabilizing factors must be accounted for, given that reports of the phenomenon are constructed by patients whose memory centers have taken hits both from pain-killing drugs and trauma. Other neurologists agree with Parnia. They claim larger-scaled investigations, into a phenomenon that may help us shed valuable light on our understanding of consciousness, are warranted.

The line in the sand almost all of them dare not cross, is to disconnect human consciousness from the brain as its main originator and master. "When you speak to experience—human experience—you're speaking about the brain," asserts neurologist Kevin Nelson. He appears to regard the possibility of any form of human consciousness disconnected from the brain as an absurdity and oxymoron.[40] Those who agree these experiences demand further investigation, insist the first place to study is the physiological and psychological processes of the brain.

Countering Parnia's assertion—meaning the history of science has been one of continually shifting and rebuilding the

---

[40] Kevin Nelson, Peter Fenwick, Sam Parnia, and Mary Neal, "Experiencing Death: An Insider's Perspective" (panel presentation, New York Academy of Sciences, December 11, 2013), 4.

framework, allowing scientists to function toward the realm of truth and reality—neurologists insist such a process has been incremental. Therefore, reshaping takes place by the gradual accretion of new knowledge on the shape of the old. They also add, those who suggest a consciousness can be separate from brain activity have zero evidentiary basis to propel their theory forward.

Parnia, when asked directly how long human consciousness can exist after the death of the brain, insists it may be a few minutes or fifty hours. He concedes, no one knows for sure how long it takes. It requires further studies.[41] Some proponents of prioritizing the revolutionary importance of the NDE/OBE phenomenon, do approach it from a much more theological perspective. They seek to build a bridge between modern science and the eschatological elements in the ancient religious texts. One such writer, Dr. Jeffrey Long, ensures that readers become aware of this bridge-building from the moment they pick up his first book, titled *Evidence of the Afterlife: The Science of Near-Death Experiences.* Long and similar writers use interviews and analyses of thousands of individuals who have undergone NDEs to make extraordinary claims, going much further than Parnia and like-minded scientists. These claims, however, can be easily rebutted by more experienced scientists; that is, if their point of view is not ignored as quackery.

---

[41] Sam Parnia. 2013. *Erasing Death* (New York: HarperCollins), 225.

Setting out seemingly strict scientific criteria for choosing his subjects, Long asserts there is life after death, based on the similarities of experience his subjects reported, including encountering a bright light, passing through a tunnel, meeting with long-deceased loved ones, and feeling the sense of alteration of time and dimension.[42]

His 2016 follow-up book is titled *God and the Afterlife*. In it, Long takes the natural next step. He claims to have scientific proof of the existence of God through comparative analyses of reports from those who met the Almighty or Jesus. Long says they all seem to have met the same deities based on similarities in the descriptions.

Parnia and other NDE researchers bemoan the difficulty of obtaining funding or grants for studies of the NDE phenomenon. It may be that writers such as Long are at fault. In his effort to reach a wider audience, through making claims they most want to hear, his books are aligned more to psychology and the emotions than hard science. This is unfortunate, because some of the evidence he unwittingly uncovers in his exhaustive interviews, and the faux-scientific prerequisites he sets for choosing subjects, could be used to shed light on the experience of the moments leading to death and transformations in consciousness. For example, the experience of heightened consciousness, which those who go through NDEs

---

[42] Jeffrey Long. 2010. *Evidence of the Afterlife* (New York: HarperCollins), 4.

report, may point to powers in the brain that are not yet fully understood.

Scientists, in fact, replicated such a heightened consciousness in laboratory rats in the moments leading up to death, in a research study conducted in the United States, published in the *Proceedings of the National Academy of Science.*[43] The report concluded in the thirty-second interval after the rats suffered cardiac arrest, high-frequency brain waves spiked to such a degree that the brain became even more active than in the fully alert stage. Such a heightened form of consciousness is not hallucinatory in nature. Instead, the study explains a stage in which a fire of impulses is raging through the brain and the senses become hyperaware. This leads to intensified visual perceptions of light and more deeply felt emotions.

The suggestion that such increased brain activity, if it also occurs in humans, could lead to an existence of consciousness as reported is fascinating. Understandably this is a leap. The human brain is a much more complex organ than that of rats. Moreover, this type of heightened reality may feel otherworldly and separate from the more banal reality as experienced by normal consciousness.

---

[43] Jimo Borjigin, UnCheol Lee, Tiecheng Liu, Dinesh Pal, Sean Huff, Daniel Klarr, Jennifer Sloboda, Jason Hernandez, Michael M. Wang, and George A. Mashour. 2013. "Surge of neurophysiological coherence and connectivity in the dying brain." *PNAS* 110 (35): 14432–14437.

It is specious, however, to assert that because such heightened consciousness is infrequent and rare, it is therefore separate from the brain. Given such experiments cannot be ethically performed on human subjects, we may never know.

Neuroscientists also countered that OBEs also occur in those not in danger of death. This occurrence is not as rare as many think. Similar experiences can be caused by diseases that cause degeneration in certain regions of the brain, sleep disorders, or losing and regaining consciousness through simple hyperventilation. Many of the experiences reported by those who undergo NDEs, in fact, can be replicated artificially by sending electrical impulses to certain regions of the brain.

NDEs may also lack the kind of definite scientific exactitude necessary for unbiased experiments. Advances in technology and CPR allow patients who, no more than a few decades before, would have been considered beyond the help of medical treatment. Now they can be sustained by life-support machines until the family decides otherwise. Those who suffer severe heart failure, once the very definition of death, can now be "resuscitated" or "revived" using techniques becoming more commonplace and effective. Doctors can go beyond trying to restart the heart to cooling the body, minimizing damage caused in the interval to the brain and other organs.

These advances have made the very definition of the moment of death so fuzzy in certain cases, such as after heart failure, that the language we use for the medical procedures are still trapped in an earlier era. If a patient is "revived" or "resuscitated," the semantic implication is the patient died when the heart stopped beating. However, given the rapidity of medical advances and improvement of techniques, such resuscitations may become so commonplace and successful that medical personnel may be considered neglectful if they fail to execute them effectively. Curiously enough, as of today, even in the best hospitals in the most advanced health care systems in the world, there is no standardized regulation and enforcement on how long emergency medical personnel must perform CPR. It is left entirely to the discretion of the doctor leading the medical team, based on his personal evaluation of the condition of the patient.

The new advance of cooling down the body to prevent damage to the brain has made such decisions even more complicated. This has created an even fuzzier benchmark of when a doctor should declare a patient beyond saving. Additionally, the decision of when a patient may suffer permanent brain damage, even if the heart begins to beat, is nothing but an educated guess. Many other variables come into play concerning the patient's history and makeup which could be unknown to some doctors, and there are mysteries of individual variances in recovery that science has not deciphered.

This shifting border between the dead and living, created by medical advances, allows those with questionable agendas to take an NDE and tailor it to their purposes. Some, like Long, do it in a nakedly opportunistic manner and with the gall of a charlatan to prove the existence of a God who doesn't need to be proven in such terms.

Others, such as Parnia, are sincere, well intentioned, and undeniably correct in their assertions that, if humankind were to have dismissed and suppressed every challenge to the current scientific framework of reality, we would still be living in caves. Still, there is a recklessness, arrogance, and even hint of opportunism—though much more eloquently disguised—in the way he summons the ghosts of revolutionary scientific minds as a shield to protect his flimsy inferences. The experience of patients undergoing a still-imperfect medical treatment may be the key to unlocking not only the most profound secrets of human consciousness, but also a better understanding of the unknown—the world beyond death.

I imagined my search for a clear scientific study to prove the existence of the soul would be quixotic at best. I realize science is very much of this world, the senses, and the perceptible. It bemused, somewhat disturbed, and startled me, when I found that some writers, such as Long, had not only donned the scientific mantle to prove the existence of an eternal soul, but that they had been more quixotic than Don Quixote himself. They attempted to prove the existence of God, ignoring the forces of faith and belief. They even demoted the revelations of religious and philosophical texts, as if they had nothing to do with such an entity. I could easily dismiss the scholarship of such refined hustlers and their almost comically dubbed foundations and institutes of NDEs.

Admittedly, writers such as Parnia held my interest through the eloquence with which they present their mysteries and how these lacunae dovetail with some concerns of my investigation. What if our consciousness is not only *of* this world but can exist beyond it? What if we have been indoctrinated to perceive the world a certain way and those beliefs blind us to other possibilities?

The sublime echoes and forceful humanity of such questions, however, vanished for me with a closer examination of the work of writers such as Parnia. I examined how he takes the mystery of the unknowable and diminishes it through a process that is almost exclusively concerned with some romantic ideal of the great scientist. In his work there is little concern with the pursuit of clarity and knowledge of great science.

Curiously enough, this scientific inquiry may yield some useful evidence—such as the heightened states of consciousness before death, as confirmed in rats. This will no doubt prove useful as we try to bridge the gap between the scientific curiosity, intent on plunging into the mystery of this world, and the more eschatological questions which lead to mysteries not just beyond this world, but beyond time and space.

The sacred texts we have examined were intended to set the scene and prepare us for our existence beyond death. They also serve to establish the given that there is such existence through its unbreakable connection to who we are in this world. The fountainhead for such otherworldly conceptions is the most natural and common occurrence in our world, the continual demise and death of all living things. The processes that drive the cycle of life, degeneration, and death are central to all scientific inquiry for the human experience. The methods of science are ill-equipped to trespass much beyond the moment of death, even if recent advances have made those boundaries fuzzier.

The next chapter will use revelations from science, the sacred texts, and eyewitness experiences. The investigation is designed to shed light on the moment when the investigation of worldly mystery ends, and the revelation of religious mystery begins.

Chapter 5

Last Life and First Death

We understand nothing of the works of God unless we take it as a principle that He wishes to blind some and to enlighten others.

-Blaise Pascal

Among the most relevant scientific discoveries of those studying NDEs has been the state of consciousness in the moments in which the body passes from the living to the dead. Due to ethical and moral strictures that regulate scientific research, however, such evidence remains anecdotal and "after the fact." It cannot be collected from controlled experiments, like those done on rats, in the experiment mentioned previously.

Keeping the discussion rooted in the physiological processes that accompany death allows us to determine where the heightened stage of awareness asserts itself more often. We can see how that awareness is connected to the physical passage from life to death. We may learn about the possibility of existence of consciousness after death. Only by pinpointing unexplainable phenomena along this trajectory can we seek to begin to unravel these mysteries.

We should be aware that continuing medical advances will expand our knowledge of each of these stages from physiological, cellular, and chemical viewpoints. Such advances may even cleave some of these stages into two or more sub-stages, further complicating how we think about the passage from life to death. We will also question how to distinguish personhood in respect to the life of the corporeal body and the existence of a consciousness associated with it.

We must accept two things in such an examination:

(1) The shifting frontiers in how we legally and philosophically define the moment of death.

(2) The accompanying conclusions that can be made depending on our perspective from the landscape of shifting frontiers.

Aside from NDEs, we need to also consider the validity of deathbed experiences. We must consider the evidence they provide of that specific stage in which an individual has similar visions but is still conscious, still completely alive, but about to pass from this world. Such experiences have been classified by some scientists as mere hallucinations, but the consistency of their occurrence across cultures, traditions, and ages, suggests something more. Recent scientific studies on the hyperactive and superiorly aware state of the brain, in the moments immediately following and preceding clinical death, may also offer a clue to what is happening with humans at this stage.

Let's examine the basic stages in the lengthy biological process, from healthy to the point where there is zero medical capability to "resuscitate" the body. This takes into consideration that at some point, we may develop to a level where it is necessary to add even more stages to what is now considered complete cellular death of the entire organism.

The first of these stages is what is popularly known as the death throes of the physical body. Also called the agonal stage, this is caused by convulsions emanating from spasms of both the voluntary and involuntary muscular system. This is also known as the famous death rattle because the individual loses control of normal breathing rhythms and gasps for air.[44] While such symptoms were more frequently reported in the past, given the current state of medical care in which most patients are heavily medicated during this stage, a more common occurrence today involves less ominous versions of the death throes.

During the days or hours leading to death, many individuals experience deathbed visions that include some of the same elements and details of NDEs. According to cardiologist Pin van Lommel, the main difference between the two experiences is, "the dying person experiences waking consciousness during the deathbed vision, and can discuss the enhanced and nonlocal consciousness at about the same time as they experience it."[45] The transcendent quality of such experiences cannot be explained by the introduction of pain-relieving opiates to the dying. They occur just as frequently in

---

[44] Sherwin B. Nuland. 1994. *How We Die* (New York: Alfred A. Knopf), 121–122.

[45] Pin van Lommel. 2010. *Consciousness Beyond Life: The Science of the Near-Death Experience* (New York: HarperCollins), 512.

individuals who are not on such drugs. Moreover, they have been copiously reported in times before these medical practices were common.

In spite of all this obstinacy, in rigorous study of the phenomenon of these visions, little has been yielded by way of their significance or evidence to contradict the consensus that they are hallucinations. It is entirely possible that consciousness is so transformed at these moments that it is granted a kind of access it has never had. Deathbed visions also take place over extended periods of time, as opposed to the brevity of ordinary hallucinations.

As in all the other stages, research on this stage of the transition from life to death allows those who study the biology of death to break this down into sub-stages. The first sub-stage involves the irreversible failure of some vital organs, such as kidneys or the liver. This in turn leads to the failure of all the rest of the vital organs, eventually including the heart, brain, and lungs. Now, when we say "irreversible," given the advances of organ transplant and life-support systems, it does not mean the patient has to die because of failure of certain vital organs; rather, if such failures are not addressed through either a transplant or artificial means, then the process of death begins.

Only after the failure of the vital systems do the non-vital systems, such as the sensory organs and muscular system, begin to collapse. This collapse is the primary cause of the convulsions, noises, and agony we associate with death throes.[46] After such a failure, specifically when the heart stops beating and vital oxygen is no longer available to the brain, the second stage, or what we know as clinical death, sets in.

Regarding consciousness, most researchers agree, in the late stage, all consciousness is still controlled solely by the chemical processes of the brain. There is activity in the neocortex, which controls most of the processes of personality, memory, and thought.[47] As we shall see, when some individuals experience NDEs, one of the more common distinctions they make from other experiences is the clarity of the memory and its untransmutable nature, despite the passing of time. This is unlike all other memories, which are tempered, made fuzzier, or simply altered, depending on certain psychological and temporal conditions. With deathbed visions, this durability is expressed in their length of time, and their continuity.

Depending on the type of death, this process can be shortened. Death by severe trauma, in which the two middle sub-stages happen instantly or not at all, is one such example.[48] At times, when the failure of a vital organ such as the heart is sudden and severe, the process can also be extremely condensed. On occasion,

---

[46] Sherwin B. Nuland. 1994. *How We Die* (New York: Alfred A. Knopf), 218–219.

[47] C. Machado. 1999. "Consciousness as a definition of death: its appeal and complexity." *Clinical Electroencephalography* 30(4):156–64.

[48] Sherwin B. Nuland. 1994. *How We Die* (New York: Alfred A. Knopf), 17–18.

seemingly healthy individuals have been seen publicly as they suffered sudden organ failure. The moment such failure affects the non-vital organs, individuals appear as if their consciousness has been transferred to a different existence just before the flip of their eyes, the minor convulsions, and loss of muscle control. This is likely simply a condensed and less intense version of the common death throes, in which the failure of such systems is more prolonged and impactful. There seems to be little to learn about the shift in consciousness from these rare examples of the moments between life and death. The individual, while seemingly in a trance, does not report anything witnessed such as near-death or deathbed experiences. Witnessing or recording such events has been futile in relation to furthering research.

The second major stage in the process of biological death is what is commonly known as clinical death.[49] This occurs when the heart stops beating and breathing ceases. Since oxygen can no longer travel to the vital organs, there is a limited amount of time people can survive during this stage, without irreversible damage. Given the advances in CPR, and the more recent developments in which cooling the body prevents permanent damage from setting in as quickly as before, much of the literature regarding near-death comes from phenomena that transpire at this point or during the following stage. Given all the medical interventions, the variable

---

[49] Ibid., 121–123.

practical definitions of "permanent" death have previously taken root to describe this juncture. From this definition of clinical death, we move on to what many neurologists proclaim as the real death: death of the brain.

Regarding our investigation of human consciousness and the self, a few factors are important to mention, to circumscribe the phenomenon of brain death. The first factor pertains to the two modes in which such a death is mentioned. The second factor concerns a philosophical confrontation with the reality that the body, and its other vital functions, can be kept going through artificial means for an indeterminate amount of time, after the brain has stopped functioning. A third factor should take into account all the unknowns about the workings of the brain, even at a surface level, and how many new discoveries are made every year, to say nothing about the workings of the deep brain at levels that we may not even know exist.

That is, when we say a person is brain dead, we say this, given the technology we have to measure activity in the brain and knowledge we have of the brain and its functions. Without a doubt, of all the vital organs in the human body, the brain is the one we know the least about. For example, it is the diseases of the brain, such as Parkinson's or Alzheimer's, which are the ones that most baffle pathologists and epidemiologists.

Researchers have mostly focused on those moments when individuals are considered brain dead, and are then resuscitated, to isolate the self or mind from the brain. In this manner, the ephemeral entities we consider the self and the soul are separated from the biological and chemical processes of the brain. Part of the problem with truly investigating such phenomena is pinpointing a definition of brain death. As far as we know, in the body such expiration does not take place instantly, rather it occurs in a set of sub-stages. There may be other stages we are not aware of yet.

For the purpose of studying human consciousness, the first stage involves the cessation of activity in the neocortex. Researchers, such as Parnia, use this criterion to classify brain death. This makes sense on a surface level, given that the functions of the neocortex involve much of what we define as consciousness. On the other hand, some researchers classify brain death strictly as the irreversible functions of all areas of the brain, including the stem. The problem many neurologists see in the work of researchers such as Parnia, is they are too hastily associating consciousness as separate from the brain, yet other areas of the brain might be still fully functioning. Since the individual is fully conscious during deathbed visions, this is not the problem.

The question of a transcendent consciousness is not that it is separated from the brain. The issue is that, while still relying on the neurochemical processes of the brain, the individual's perception may have lifted the veil of a world beyond quotidian consciousness and perhaps peered into the afterlife. Such empowered consciousness is relevant to this investigation because of its power to witness a reality beyond the life of the body.

However, if the conditions under which Parnia studies his subjects persist for a certain period of time after cardiac arrest, and with a complete lack of oxygen to the brain, complete brain death will eventually occur. This biological death is the next main stage of death; in it all vital organs of the body are irreversibly dead. They cannot be revived, even by using artificial means. Even at this stage, there is still life at the cellular level of the organism. The amount of time of remaining cellular life varies according to the external conditions that affect the body and its biological history. The last stage of death, as we currently define it, is complete death, even at the most minute cellular level. It may not fully occur until the biological matter of the individual transforms into something we don't recognize as a person.[50]

Given the shifting quality of what we consider life, it is no surprise that the frontiers shift with medical advances. Our philosophical consensus of what we consider a person, consciousness, and life itself, as it relates to an individual and human consciousness is another determining factor. Before we let the scientific perception of this phenomenon go entirely, in relation to our investigation of the life after death, we should permit another obstacle to our investigation. The very term "life after death" is, in

---

[50] Ibid., 77–78.

some ways, the paragon of oxymora, pointing to the fact that we are performing an investigation about a phenomenon that our language resists as a possibility. This is perhaps why researchers are attracted to reports of NDEs that, as of yet, seem to defy scientific explanations. They want to break through this barrier that even common semantics resists. The problem is they run into the same difficulties as poets, mythmakers, and linguists: they are trying to conceive of something beyond our world using the tools and scales of this world.

As we attempt to build a bridge between the work of scientists studying consciousness, and the religious revelations at the heart of what we consider faith, let's examine one of Parnia's most famous cases.

Mary Neal was a woman in her late fifties who, during a kayaking trip, careened over a waterfall and plummeted under the surface of the pool below. She was submerged under water for over fifteen minutes. Neal went into cardiac arrest and was resuscitated after more than half an hour.[51] After she regained consciousness, she reported an NDE particular to her. Her experience was unique. She returned to her body with a calling to share the experience with others. [52]

---

[51] Mary C. Neal. 2001. *To Heaven and Back* (Colorado Springs, CO: WaterBrook Press), 57–58.
[52] Ibid., 135–137.

Neal became a modern-day prophet because of her revelation. She considered herself as transformed as the reports of the transformation of Paul at Damascus or the many others who have had similar spiritual revelations.

Neal's memoir *To Heaven and Back* is primarily distinguishable from other such works because of the scientific rigor with which Neal examines her experience and uses it as a foundation for the examination of other such experiences on record. As an orthopedic spine surgeon, Neal does not have to try hard to assert her scientific chops. Examinations of a personal experience from an individual trained to think as a scientist adds credibility to her experience. Reading her accounts, there is no doubt Neal considers what happened outside the range of her scientific knowledge. This is particularly true in what she considers the quality and nature of the recollection:

> It is entirely qualitatively different from any other experience—dream, hallucination, or big event in your life. Such is true of the persistent "realness" as felt by the observer. In near-death experiences, it is a qualitatively different type of memory, so it's really not a recollection. That's one of the things that is interesting from a physiologic standpoint, because indeed the brain cells start to disintegrate—start to burst; there's no way those

brain cells are forming memories. If you look at the studies that were done trying to replicate the hallucinatory effect of a near-death experience, there are similarities when the neurotransmitters are injected, but the memory, again, is qualitatively different—it is not a near-death experience. These are not recollections. I remember the day my son was killed very clearly, but I know that if I were to tell the experience of that day, every couple of years for the rest of my life, the details would change a little bit, but everyone's description of a near-death experience remains exactly the same, no matter how much time has passed.[53]

This distinction is important, considering the nature of such experiences, as opposed to the recollections of memories and experiences, to what has been considered religious revelation. However, as soon as Neal begins to qualify the "realness" of an experience, granting privilege and importance to an event based on something so difficult to define, she has removed her scientist's white coat and donned the robe of a philosopher. The focus on persistence makes sense. The experience led Neal, a scientist, to

---

[53] Kevin Nelson, Peter Fenwick, Sam Parnia, and Mary Neal, "Experiencing Death: An Insider's Perspective" (panel presentation, New York Academy of Sciences, December 11, 2013), 12.

unquestionably define the moment of death as the instance that "spirit leaves the body." Accounts such as hers may serve as a bridge from the scientific investigations of these events to similar moments expressed in religious texts.

After reviewing the idea of death in ancient texts in search of proof of the immaterial soul, examining stories, and investigating people who are dying or who have had NDEs, I cannot claim to have found any irrefutable evidence one way or another. Admittedly, this may be because there are aspects of death we do not yet understand. Ultimately, the religious and unscientific explanation of the afterlife is not convincing for lack of proof.

Based on my research and limited knowledge, my conclusion, given all that we have examined, is: death is the end. Science has not established proof otherwise, partly because of a willing reluctance to pursue the issue. This leaves me resigned to the somewhat daunting conclusion that religious conceptions of the afterlife may just be fairy tales. Obviously, science has not delved into the biology and metaphysics of death deeply enough since it is concerned foremost with life.

Yet another look at the sacred texts from the purging undergone through scientific analyses of the topic may be just the critical shock this investigation requires.

PART TWO : THE PERCEPTION

Chapter 6

The Relapse

We don't know a millionth of one percent about anything.

-Thomas Edison

After reviewing all the material covered, I began to suspect I might have taken the wrong direction. I sought to reexamine what had already been studied, in hopes of finding a new direction to ultimately put me back on the right path. After analyzing various conceptions of death in the ancient books, searching for proof of the immaterial soul, examining stories related to both, and investigating cases involving those who are dying or who have had NDEs, I couldn't find any evidence that proved life after death conclusively. This was one of the essential conditions of my search. The evidence must not be flimsy or poetically justified.

In the dissatisfaction I felt about these initial conclusions, I also began to suspect I had fallen short of another primary condition imposed on the investigation: I would accept any of the results of the search, as long as they were arrived at in a sincere and unbiased manner. As I reviewed the material again, reaffirming my pledge to abide by the initial conditions, I became as curious of the source of my dissatisfaction as I was committed to return to the sacred texts without letting such dissatisfaction bias my readings and interpretations.

First, I had to put the scientific research aside, while not abandoning the insights it lent. Admittedly, some of the research on the phenomenon of NDEs and deathbed experiences is still in its infancy. It may yet produce more conclusive results, as it plunges ever deeper into this still-little-explored country of human existence.

Until such a time, we are left with the religious, unscientific explanation for the afterlife that, for our purposes, has not proven convincing enough without ultimate proof. Based on the comprehensive—and somewhat circumscribed—examination of the sacred texts and our predetermined guidelines, we must come to terms with the most logical and likely conclusion: Death marks the end of individual existence. The strict and unflinching analyses undertaken in the discussions, up to this point, unmask the religious myths. You see, no matter how grandly presented or poetically evoked, they appear to be nothing more than fairy tales and wish-fulfillment fantasies, in the face of oblivion.

However, given the unavoidably limited extent of my initial examination of these texts, I decided to eliminate the potential for errors, oversights, or misreading. I gave a final look at the ancient books, suspecting it wouldn't change the initial conclusion, remaining vigilant to nuances, resisting reductive dismissals, and not closing doors on any new discoveries. Given the broad and harsh judgment of my conclusion, the sacred texts deserved to be heard.

Since the Quran is the most recent of the books, and claims to be the last revelation from God, the most effective appeal had to lie hidden in this "closing argument." A part of me also knew that, since this was the text I was most familiar with, any revisionist argument had to begin from my area of expertise. I tried to ignore the windstorm and drenching rain of the night on which I began reviewing certain crucial verses in the Quran. After all, far be it for me to believe this was some sign connected to the nature of my endeavor.

Such superstitious reactions went against the spirit of the predetermined guidelines and conditions of the process. Given that humans have long assigned personal characteristics to the impersonal natural world, particularly in moments where much is at stake, I was hardwired by thousands of years of such practices to react to nature as if it sat in judgment of me and my ilk, mankind. The rain pounding on my rooftop and the wind howling through the crevices of my windows became, in some area of my brain, prone to expressionist hysterics. These were the cries of man himself against the irrevocable conclusion that he was condemned to eternal oblivion.

How often, in the face of the most violent eruptions of the natural world, have humans proclaimed the end of the world? Yet, what they were more precisely proclaiming was the end of their time and the doom of their little corner of the universe. Not to mention the death of the frail body. Time, we know, goes on and galaxies continue to expand. In the Quran, such disorientation and misinterpretation of the passage of time, caused by a lack of perspective, is shown in the confusion of those who have been raised on the Day of Judgment:

> And the Horn will be blown; and at once from the graves to their Lord they will hasten. They will say, "O woe to us! Who has raised us up from our sleeping place?" [The reply will be] "This is what the Most Merciful had promised, and the messengers told the truth."54

The baffled query of the newly raised, "Who has raised us up from our sleeping place?" This suggests these beings lack as much awareness of being dead as a sleeper being in a state of sleep. Some Islamic scholars point to these verses when casting doubt on the existence of an immaterial soul. Here, the dead are represented as sleepers who have no awareness of their state or the passing of time. This is dramatized by the befuddlement of the sleepers after they are resurrected on the Day of Judgment. This contradicts other verses I cited earlier in chapter three, which clearly refer to consciousness that passes from one realm to another, at the moment of death.

To reach a satisfactory interpretation of this verse in the Quran, in light of other material cited, I read it repeatedly, sometimes very fast from beginning to end, sometimes at a glacial pace, trying to absorb the meaning of each individual phrase, each

---

54 Sura 36:51–52.

word. Eventually, through a combination of the trancelike state induced by repetition, and the dissociation produced by taking something apart, it felt like I were reading the material for the first time. No, it was more forceful and memorable than that. It was both as if I were reading a passage that I had never read before, and as if, in some other realm, I had memorized the passage long ago. I felt as if I could recite it fully after only reading it once. I had been looking through a grimy window before and, in one stroke, the window turned pellucid.

Such revelation led me to sharpen my focus. I remained open-minded to new and divergent interpretations of death as described by the Quran. Some of these proved to be at odds with traditional Islamic dogma. They may have been elaborations on other religious interpretations of life after death. In these verses, the Quran does not refer to an immaterial soul after death. It doesn't even address the nothingness of oblivion. Instead, death is simply expressed as the absence of consciousness, which is only granted back to the individual on the day of resurrection.

At such a time, sleepers regain awareness and individual consciousness. Terms that allude to time will become more compromised and ineffective tools with which to delve into the nature of pre- and post-time existences. This means the moment of death is the first step in the process of resurrection. In other words, death is the time travel of consciousness.

Death is not an all-out assault on our temporal existence, but it is a good slap in its face. It suspends the rules of time and space. Popular culture interprets the "space" of the world after the resurrection as a scene with angels floating like astronauts inside a space station. However, beyond that vision, things remain foggy. The passage of time, in the post-resurrection realm, is even more complicated. It is strenuous to conceive, given the only metaphorical conceit we can borrow is time frozen, or the pause button. The suspension of time is a much more radical and apocalyptic proposition than it may at first seem. The very type of revelation we commonly associate with adopting a new perspective, or the insight that expands our awareness, may also be a self-imploding force. It condemns all to oblivion unless it strikes at the exact moment of death or beyond. Looking at verses with particular attention to such references, we understand death as the greatest revelation of all. By liberating us from its snares, death empowers us to fully comprehend the actions of our life and their repercussions, for the first time. Through death, the Quran suggests, an individual is freed from the shackles of time and its monotonous and tyrannical linearity:

> [For such is the state of the disbelievers], until,
> when death comes to one of them, he says, "My
> Lord, send me back, That I might do righteousness
> in that which I left behind." No! It is only a word

he is saying; and behind them is a barrier until the

Day they are resurrected.[55]

The revelation forces the individual to come to terms with the whole life in a "condition" in which wholeness is a prelude to resurrection. Wholeness suggests the entire individual and not just the consciousness. This revelation remains hypothetical from our perspective in this world. It is impossible really, even as it shifts toward a more profound and nuanced understanding that sheds light on the truth, and purpose of a life, through overcoming the barrier of our perceptions of ourselves as creatures inseparable from the past, present, and future:

And the intoxication of death will bring the truth;
that is what you were trying to avoid. And the
Horn will be blown. That is the Day of [carrying
out] the threat.[56]

Additionally, this passage intimates, such an intoxication is the necessary foundation for the resurrection to come on the Day of Judgment. We cannot be resurrected without experiencing death. This seems self-explanatory, but in the way we try to conceive of the afterlife through language and conceits of this world, we paint ourselves into a corner. These passages in the Quran portray the

---

[55] Sura 23:99–100.
[56] Sura 50:19–20.

moment of death. It is not portrayed through referencing an immaterial world and non-corporeal soul on its journey there, or one trapped in some other dimension. It is shown as a physical and mental awakening into an impossible realm. The consciousness of the deceased does not detach from the body per se, but rather pries loose from the binds of time and begins to experience reality in such a purged state. Additionally, after the resurrection, the nontemporal essence of this new state disorients and confuses the newly resurrected. The variations and distinctions on the passing of time have become moot:

> He will say, "How long did you remain in earth in number of years?" They will say, "We remained a day or part of a day; ask those who enumerate." He will say, "You stayed not but a little – if only you had known. Then did you think that We created you uselessly and that to Us you would not be returned?"[57]

A crucial revelation, at the end of this passage, stresses the absurdity of human beings thinking they would leave the world in any other state but the one they entered it, that is, as a corporeal being. Freed from linear time, the individual's consciousness is also stripped of the one entity it imagined intrinsic to its very existence,

---

[57] Sura 23:112–115.

the passing of time in a body with an expiration date. As such, the dead exit the earthly realm, which is controlled on all levels, by the passing of time. After exiting, they can enter another physical realm.

> And the Day the Hour appears the criminals will
> swear they had remained but a moment. Thus,
> they were deluded. But those who were given
> knowledge and faith will say, "You remained the
> extent of Allah's decree until the Day of
> Resurrection, and this is the Day of Resurrection,
> but you did not used to know."[58]

Under the ultimate decree of God, this world is beyond human constructs, which were dependent on universal time. Such constructs include human language and science. As subversive as this interpretation of the verses may seem, it was perceived as being just as dangerous and portentous during the time of the Prophet. Many verses in the Quran portray unbelievers accusing Muhammad and other prophets with madness and deceit. One of the biggest reasons for these accusations is the promise of an immediate physical resurrection at the moment of death:

> But those who disbelieve say, "Shall we direct you
> to a man who will inform you [that] when you
> have disintegrated in complete disintegration, you

---

[58] Sura 30:55–56.

are [recreated] in a new creation? Has he invented about Allah a lie or is there in him madness?" Rather, they who do not believe in the Hereafter will be in the punishment and [are in] extreme error.[59]

The extreme error committed by doubters arises from the simple mistake of binding God to the forces that bind human beings and turn their body to dust—the passing of time. At a loss, the doubters even challenge the prophet to prove his truth by revealing to them their dead ancestors:

> And when Our verses are recited to them as clear evidences, their argument is only that they say, "Bring [back] our forefathers, if you should be truthful." Say, "Allah causes you to live, then causes you to die; then He will assemble you for the Day of Resurrection, about which there is no doubt, but most of the people do not know."[60]

People are unaware of the reality of their existence. They have not yet been purged and intoxicated with truth, which (to bastardize the poet John Keats) is and can only be death, just as death is and can only be truth.[61] Such doubters have a limited

---

[59] Sura 34:7–8.
[60] Sura 45:25–26.
[61] John Keats, "On Death."

understanding using their earthly tools made to engage the issues and conflicts of temporal forces. Even mankind's most powerful tool, language, is earthly, and thus incapable of providing true revelation.

All prophets mentioned in the Quran warned their people about the coming resurrection in the Day of Judgment. People remained ignorant of the wisdom of the prophets. Instead, they demanded they bring to pass what had been promised, as if God was supposed to act at the command of his prophets. To reveal to the people the drastic error of such irreverence and lack of faith, Earth's forces were turned against its inhabitants. Such disruptions and eruptions in the natural cycles heralded the Day of Judgment, in which nature itself and its accomplice, linear time, would be disrupted.

> They said, "Have you come to delude us away
> from our Gods? Then bring us what you promise
> us if you should be of the truthful." He said,
> "Knowledge [of its time] is only with Allah, and I
> convey to you that with which I was sent; but I see
> you [to be] a people behaving ignorantly." And
> when they saw it as a cloud approaching their
> valleys, they said, "This is a cloud bringing us
> rain!" Rather, it is that for which you were
> impatient: a wind, within it a painful punishment.[62]

---

[62] Sura 46:22–24.

An expression to show the punishment of the Day of Judgment has been brought inside the cloud, as if these heavy clouds act as a gate to the promised resurrection. In a similar analogy, the Quran broadens our understanding of the very phenomenon of death by referring to previous death experiences. If nothingness is something we can feel and remember, we should be able to feel all the millions of years of nonexistence before earthly life.

The Quran calls that period of time before earthly life "Death," so an individual with no physical existence will not feel time from the beginning till the day of their firstborn. They will have no awareness of such a state outside of the scope of earthly existence.[63] To such a state, the individual returns at the end of his or her earthly life and before the start of a new life.

> How can you disbelieve in Allah when you were lifeless, and He brought you to life; then He will cause you to die, then He will bring you [back] to life, and then to Him you will be returned.[64]

In such meaning, the verses I have cited in Chapter 3 can now be understood differently. For example, the verse "…And if you could but see when the wrongdoers are in the overwhelming pangs of death while the angels extend their hands, [saying], 'Discharge your souls! Today you will be awarded the punishment

---

[63] Sura 67:2.
[64] Sura 2:28.

of [extreme] humiliation for what you used to say against Allah other than the truth and [that] you were, toward His verses, being arrogant.'"[65] This describes the resurrection of disbelievers at the moment of their death; the humiliation and punishment of those who disbelieved happens in their day of resurrection, not in a spiritual word. The word "soul" is not part of the original Arabic text, the original Arabic word is "*Nafes*" which is equivalent to the English word "self." Therefore, the verse can be translated to "…while the angels extend their hands, [saying], bring yourself out [from your graves] …." However, the difficulty to perceive the idea of an immediate physical resurrection at the moment of death led to interpret the verse by a spiritual existence. The word "soul" was used in the English translation of Quran to match the Islamic interpretation of this verse.

Here is where language fails, and prepositions that signal the passing of time, such as "before," "after," and "between," are as near as we can come to conceiving of such a revelation. It could be that the right word to describe this phenomenon is "death," from our limited and chained perspective.

---

[65] Sura 6:93.

Chapter 7

The Blind Angel

Such an interpretation of these newly cited verses presents a challenge to the guidelines we set up for our investigation. The evidence and analysis suggest the Quran reveals death is a delusion; it is a phase where terms such as "ending" and "beginning" become unnecessary. We must deal with the conundrum since one of the prongs in our three-pronged approach is rooted in one of the investigative and narrative disciplines that adheres to and exploits the passing of time. It is more of a tool to discovery and insight. How else can history be understood if not by looking backward? What other primary purpose can such storytelling and knowledge have but to guide us on how to move forward?

Walter Benjamin's well-known image of the angel of history[66] may be a useful one to help us evaluate the truth of the ahistorical in a historical context. As Benjamin describes his iconic image, it is a being caught between the desire to redeem the catastrophes of the past—by humans in their vicious cycle of conflict with time and the self. Further, there is the ardent yearning to return to a state where such redemption is moot—the pre-temporal innocence of mankind.

---

[66] Walter Benjamin. 2006. *Selected Writings,* Volume 4, 1938–1940 (Cambridge, MA: Belknap Press of Harvard University Press), 392.

With the human face turned toward the past, there is a chain of events to be observed. There is a single catastrophe, which keeps piling wreckage upon itself. It hurls in front of our feet. The angel would like to stay, awaken the dead, and make whole what has been smashed. A storm blows in from Paradise; it has got caught in his wings with such violence that the angel can no longer close them. This storm irresistibly propels him into a future to which his back had been turned, while the pile of debris before him grows skyward.

Caught between the temporal cataclysm of the past and the storm dragging him toward a paradisiacal future, he is snared by a barrier. He cannot get there, with his back turned. The angel is a representation of humankind. We are torn between a world controlled by time, our actions, and failures in both worlds. This is what the Quran refers to as the state of the first death before our birth. Thus, the verses reviewed in the previous chapter not only elucidate the nature of the world at the moment of death, before the resurrection, and beyond the Day of Judgment. They also shed light on mankind's tragic love affair with the sorrows of his temporal existence.

Given that revelation, like desire, is of its own moment, what we call the present is always at best just slightly beyond our reach. Trapped in time, once we have understood the nature of the present moment, it has already passed—it no longer is.

Humans are creatures chasing after their own tail (life) endlessly. We never quite catch up to it because of a tragic inability to exist in the present, the original state. Thus, we invent language, figments of the imagination, and art. We build grand towers toward the heavens, all things that create the illusion that the oppressor's draconian consequences can be evaded. The revelation cannot be lived in historical time.

These remedies are at best a temporary, if soothing, salve. Soon they make him even more aware of his failure yet to be fulfilled. Humankind, like the angel, yearns to make "whole what has been smashed,"[67] but his vainglory, in this mission, too often leads him to a cataclysm of wholesale smashing. To suggest or, even worse, "to hope" such a cycle can be escaped becomes the very definition of madness.

We are wont to think of the mad as existing in an alternate reality. In a sense, they have escaped, but only by forfeiting through trauma, dread, stress, chemical interactions, or some other means. Madness gives us the courage to cast off the awareness that this moment is the present and now it is not present . . . not, present . . . not, and so on, ad infinitum. The infinite failures in the zillion battles against taming time mark the individual married to the cause of human fulfillment as a zealot, after so many tours of duty reflexively continuing the fight, even after the war has ended.

The escape of madness may mimic revelation. Let's call it a devolution of consciousness, an early surrender. The purging

---

[67] Ibid.

brought on by death, and extrication of our habitual instinct to chase after the present, at best always half a step out of reach, can truly expand awareness so consciousness rises and syncs with God's decree. However, this is the world that, according to all sacred texts, has been created for human existence. Through their actions in this world, they will be pleased or disappointed.

Human beings turn both personally and collectively to the past in shame, resignation, and unwavering desire. They may have a limited understanding, sublime efforts to rise above their base temporality. It's all they have. They cannot ever live in the present fully. Each future, even one that is seconds away, is infinite in its possibilities and dependent on infinite variables.

We delude ourselves that this is a beast we can tame and exploit. We never realize our revision-happy memory. Biased records only create an illusion of the past. We are left with as many versions as there are heads with bowdlerized memories, compromised narratives, and narratives never told. If we tame the beast of the past, it will be a shadow-beast painted in gaudy revisionist colors, stinking of the cheap malleable material of the official story, which can be easily changed to become its opposite.

Humans continue to search in the faith they may see beyond their own invention and discover the truth. As the literary critic Terry Eagleton wrote about Benjamin's time-ensnared and wrong-way angel of history,

[i]n one of his shrewdest sayings, Benjamin
remarked that what drives men and women to
revolt against injustice is not dreams of liberated
grandchildren, but memories of enslaved
ancestors. It is by turning our gaze to the horrors
of the past, in the hope that we will not thereby be
turned to stone, that we are impelled to move
forward.[68]

Or, to phrase this in terms of the Quranic verses presented
earlier: it is only through an unflinching reenvisioning of his past,
through the release of death that human beings can come to a true
understanding of their temporal existence. Thus, they can be made
ready for a new existence under God's decree. This is a state that,
like the bliss of the present, they can never quite reach, and by its
nature they can never fully comprehend, until they dwell in it
through the passage of death. The actions of a life become the
horrors of their past. Fallen human beings continually seek to
redress and redeem these actions. This is their moral ballast. Such a
gaze only on past horrors inevitably espies new horrors. Human
beings' skills at redressing and redeeming are only an approximation
of the true redemption brought about by revelation—an educated
guess. We are limited by the very nature of temporal existence. Off

---

[68] Terry Eagleton. 2009. "Waking the Dead." *New Statesman.*

we go on a wild-goose chase we hope may lead tangentially to a state we don't remember—innocence.

Even God is confined to mimicry in this fallen world. Natural disasters, in which tectonic plates shift violently under the lives of humans, signal to the true revolution of consciousness. This revolution will come through death, resurrection, and a return to God's decree. In such a world, human beings return as they were brought in and become one with the decree again.

Much of Benjamin's poetics were pilfered from Jewish mysticism.[69] It is not surprising that his work elucidates some of the complexities that arise from a close reading of the Quranic verses. The Quran is a fulfillment of previous revelations as recorded in other sacred texts. As such, I deemed it worthwhile to return to some of the other texts, referenced in the previous chapters, to establish any relevant or missed connections.

---

[69] Adam Kirsch. 2006. "The Philosopher Stoned." *The New Yorker*.

Chapter 8

Connecting the Texts

With an understanding built on the revelation of the meaning of death in the Quran, how compatible should these new conceptions be, with scholarly consensus, regarding our secular interpretations of ancient verses? And how can we revise our readings of connected material in other sacred texts to better serve as a foundation for the deeper analysis of the Quran verses?

New Testament

I must return to the story of Jesus Christ's resurrection, which I mentioned in chapter 2. In that discussion, I established the grounds for doubts regarding the story of the physical resurrection of Jesus. Now after understanding the new meaning of death, I know, without a doubt, that the one who appeared to the disciples was a Fake Christ. The following verse may serve as textual basis for a new revelation: "But I tell you, from now on you will see the Son of Man seated at the right hand of Power and coming on the clouds of heaven."[70] In such words and similar terminology, Christ, more than once, describes what kind of resurrection he foretells. As with Muhammad, Jesus attracted accusations of madness and deceit;

---

[70] Matthew 26:63.

in fact, from a historical context, he may have been crucified for blasphemy.

> He has uttered blasphemy. What further witnesses
> do we need? You have now heard his blasphemy.
> What is your judgment?[71]

At the root of such accusations lurked the fear that he was urging his followers to cast away the old laws. He seemed to suggest they could exist under new radical concepts antithetical to the very laws of nature by which creatures survived and thrived for eons. This natural law favors the strong overpowering and abolishing the weak. The weak are exploited while the powerful become even stronger and prouder. This is expressed through the conquest of great cities and the building of giant monuments to the almighty God. The principle was followed so consistently and effortlessly one would think the laws originated with human beings themselves and not all other living things. Such a revolution in behavior could mean the undoing of humankind. No wonder Jesus was labeled a blasphemer. What would become of David and his tribe if he had turned his other cheek to Goliath?

Taking into account the revelation detailed and elaborated upon in previous chapters, and relying on verses from the New Testament, and historical analysis, I posit the conceit that, when

---

[71] Matthew 26:66–67.

Jesus talked about resurrection and the second coming "from now on you will see…heaven," he was not talking about a near coming in the life of the disciples. He wasn't even talking about something we can understand through a linear conception of time or what would be of consequence in the natural order of the world. Why would a second coming abide by the laws of a realm his teachings sought to overturn? I will show that, in fact, it is much more likely and consistent with his own sayings and sermons that Jesus was talking about a second coming beyond the reach of time (the Day of Judgment), where the disciples are resurrected and witness his coming as he promised.

To him, his crucifixion was the doorway through which he passed to the Day of Judgment. He willfully submitted to it, sometimes even against his human nature, which was also of this world, as evidenced by his hesitation in his prayers in the Garden of Gethsemane.[72] He performed this unnatural act—submission to a long torture. It was a suicide really because he could have saved himself by saying the right word countless times. Still, it was not a defeat, it was a victory. His submission was the only way he could lead his people to the path toward their own resurrection. He challenged our adherence to the dictums of the natural world. It was a simple plan, on paper, if not for its hyper-subversive

---

[72] Matthew 26:37–44.

underpinnings. All his followers had to do was follow him and he would lead them there:

> "Whoever wants to be my disciple must deny themselves and take up their cross and follow me."[73]

In a manner, these are the rules of the road for Christian believers. They are not, however, a description of the destination, which is the second coming, referred to elsewhere as the Day of Judgment. To even speak of the second coming as a destination is to entrap it in our conceptions of temporal existence. This description makes it an event that would occur in *near-time*, as interpreted by early Christians. The misconception is the fault of the limitations of our language and not revealing of, or consistent with, the nature of Jesus's prophecy.

A telling moment that reveals Jesus's rebellion against the snares of the temporal world occurs while he is still on the cross. One of the thieves crucified alongside him addresses Jesus: "He said, 'Jesus, remember me when you come into your kingdom.' And Jesus said to him, 'Truly, I say to you, today you will be with me in paradise.'"[74]

This suggests, at the moment of death, there is a resurrection and second coming already happening. It is a miracle that cannot be

---

[73] Matthew 16:24.
[74] Luke 23:42–43.

interpreted through a temporal lens because it has detached itself from such tethers. Jesus had promised his resurrection as such: "But I tell you, from now on, you will see the Son of Man seated at the right hand of Power and coming on the clouds of heaven."[75]

To the thief, he says: He would be there at the right hand of the father the very day of his death, but the allegedly resurrected Jesus appears to Mary Magdalene and the disciples three days later.[76] This is not confusion on Jesus's part and doesn't directly disprove the physical resurrection, but it is consistent with the conceit of a kingdom whose creator is unconcerned with the way we document the passing of time. This distinction he often asserted, most notably to Pilate, as discussed. The promises of Jesus have been fulfilled, although not in the disciples' time, nor in a near future time, but in a world unlocked from time.

Old Testament

The Old Testament describes a promised land for people of good deeds and faith, and Sheol for people of evil deeds. Again, it shows an immediate transition to that place in corporeal form. This is consistent with our reading of the Quran, and its claims of a future afterlife. In the Book of Numbers, Moses calls out two evildoers from the tents of wicked men:

---

[75] Matthew 26:63.
[76] John 20:11–18.

Moses said, "Hereby you shall know that the Lord
has sent me to do all these works . . . If these men
die as all men die, or if they are visited by the fate
of all mankind, then the Lord has not sent me. But
if the Lord creates something new, and the ground
opens its mouth and swallows them up with all
that belongs to them, and they go down alive into
Sheol, then you shall know that these men have
despised the Lord." And as soon as he had
finished speaking all these words, the ground
under them split apart. And the earth opened its
mouth and swallowed them up, with their
households and all the people who belonged to
Korah and all their goods. So, they and all that
belonged to them went down alive into Sheol, and
the earth closed over them, and they perished from
the midst of the assembly.[77]

Graphic descriptions of the fate of the wicked, as they pass
to Sheol, also appear frequently in the Book of Psalms, Daniel, and
others. Even so, the Pharisees did not accept, and could not
incorporate into their own opportunistic Scripture readings, Christ's
message and the reality of a future afterlife. Even when Jesus came
and tried to explain this to them, they turned from such readings.

---

[77] Numbers 16: 25–35.

The volatile structure during the Roman occupation and hypersensitivity to the political fragility of accords made with Roman authorities, may have caused the Pharisees to take Christ's vision literally: the heaven and the coming of the king not only in this life, but in their lifetime and on their turf.[78]

This was the only way the Romans would have taken interest and sought to persecute one of the many prophets preaching in the land. Christ must have been perceived as a political revolutionary and a threat to the stability of the Roman occupation. The Romans crucified Jesus for preaching about political rebellion, and for fomenting fantasies of usurper kings who would challenge the authority of the Pharisees, possibly planning a move against the Roman rulers.[79] Jesus clearly rejected the interpretation of his kingdom as a thing of this world. When the Pharisees tried to entrap him, asking him if they should pay taxes, Jesus asked for a coin, and showing them the image of the emperor on it responded: "Render unto Caesar the things that are Caesar's; and render unto God the things that are God's."[80] Such a stout proponent of timely tax payments hardly fits the mold of a political zealot.

According to the Quran and to the Bible, the Promised Land is not of this world; rather, the promised kingdom (heaven) is a place in a world to come.

---

[78] Luke 11:37–54.
[79] Mark 15:3.
[80] Mark 12:17.

A more extended expression of his absolute lack of interest in the accumulation of worldly power (the rotted root of linear history) occurs when the hapless Roman governor, Pontius Pilate, tries to finagle a way to not crucify a man he knows has not committed a crime under Roman law. Jesus, as in many previous occasions, has no interest in conspiring with a crooked governor to save his life, as would have been the natural instinct of most innocent people:

> Pilate entered his headquarters again and called
> Jesus and said to him, "Are you the King of the
> Jews?" Jesus answered, "Do you say this of your
> own accord, or did others say it to you about me?"
> Pilate answered, "Am I a Jew? Your own nation
> and the chief priests have delivered you over to
> me. What have you done?" Jesus answered, "My
> kingdom is not of this world. If my kingdom were
> of this world, my servants would have been
> fighting, that I might not be delivered over to the
> Jews. But my kingdom is not from the world."
> Then Pilate said to him, "So you are a king?"
> Jesus answered, "You say that I am a king. For
> this purpose, I was born and for this purpose I
> have come into the world—to bear witness to the

truth. Everyone who is of the truth listens to my voice."[81]

This bearing witness to the truth is what finally condemns Jesus to the cross. While Pilate has no interest in executing an innocent man, he has less interest in upsetting stability between the Romans and the ruling Pharisees. He does what many of us would have done: he walks away from the truth. Pilate pretends he is not to blame for the bloodthirsty madness of others by ritually washing his hands. He offers the people outside a false illusion of power by letting them decide whether the prophet or a common thief should be crucified. Pilate is the epitome of a mortal man bound in the chains of historical time. And his empty, grandiose gestures with Jesus have become emblematic of human cowardice and inaction in the face of wrong.

All other ancient books discuss life after death. This discussion is either a supporting confirmation of the Quran's and Bible's claims, or evidence of foundational myths that portray the realm of death as one in which unnatural, supernatural, or contra-natural forces exist. This makes it seem distinctly separate from earthly existence. An example can be in ancient Egyptian tombs. The tombs held treasures, gold, food, sometimes weapons, because people believed, when the dead arose, they could use them in their journey to the afterlife.

---

[81] John 18:33–37.

While humans are mortal and there is no existence of an immortal soul, the conceit of the soul was concocted to narrow the gap between the distant physical resurrection to come and the moment of death. Such a period may seem infinite from our perspective but is of no consequence in the eternal present. In ancient times, it was hard to understand the meaning of the absence of time, or that time could be relative. Conceptions about the flexibility of time are easier to grasp now, yet we still use perforce a language that cannot fully accommodate such phenomena.

This is best explained by referring to the simplest of symbols in our plane of existence when seeking to explain the unimaginable. We use a train to stand in for light in a visual explication of Einstein's famous theory. A black hole, like the one Alice fell through, allows us to imagine a place much more curious and dangerous than she could fathom. There, a flash of light is as heavy as a bowling ball. We accept such existences but must still stoop to use primitive methods of comprehension not so radically different from when the poet insisted a chariot with a God at the helm pulled the sun from the east to west.

Quran

The Holy Quran provides an interesting view of the events leading up to the crucifixion of Jesus. An Islamic interpretation of the Quran connects some of the warnings we reviewed above, in which Christ cautions his disciples about impostors. The impostor seems designed to achieve some other purpose, however. He appears before the crucifixion and not as the risen Messiah.[82] In a sense, this impostor is more a patsy, in a setup to dupe the disciples and not a would-be Messiah with maniacal motivations.

> And their saying, "Indeed, we have killed the
> Messiah, Jesus, the son of Mary, the messenger of
> Allah." And they did not kill him, nor did they
> crucify him. They were deceived. And indeed,
> those who differ over it are in doubt about it. They
> have no knowledge of it except the following
> assumption: they did not kill him for certain.
> Rather, Allah raised him to himself, and ever is
> Allah exalted and wise.[83]

Translations of these verses explain the literal "they were deceived" by adding "another was made to resemble him." So, it is a trick played on the disciples that allows God to save the prophet, as it is confirmed in another verse:

> When Allah said, "O Jesus, indeed I will take you
> and raise you to myself and purify you from those
> who disbelieve and make those who follow you

---

[82] G. C. Anawati. 2012. "Isa." In *Encyclopaedia of Islam,* second edition. Brill Online.
[83] Sura 4:157–158.

superior to those who disbelieve until the Day of the Resurrection."[84]

Most Muslim scholars interpret these verses that Jesus did not die, and God raised him from earth to heaven alive. This happens in the Gospels only after Jesus descended to hell and appeared to his disciples as resurrected from the dead.[85] The scenario in the Quran presents a problem for my argument of the resurrected body in the Day of Judgment. The ruse that may have been played on the disciples after the crucifixion is understood as a denial of the physical death of Jesus as a mortal.

There is another translation, which corresponds with the Bible and supports my argument. It addresses the contradictions on a literal level. For instance, in the verse above, the phrase "I will raise you to myself and purify you" means "I will let you die and purify you." But in an honorable way.[86]

These variants on the translation address how God expresses his will through the actions of those whom God creates. The expression of such volition may be taken literally, linearly, and historically, in the time of human beings. It also works figuratively, in the conception of God from human being's limited understanding.

---

[84] Sura 3:55.
[85] Luke 24:36.
[86] The Monotheist Group. 2008. *The Message – A Translation of the Glorious Qur'an* (Brainbow Press).

Not all verses in the Holy Quran can be taken literally. Sometimes, the actions of human beings, historical events per se, are a figurative expression of God's will. For example,

> And you did not kill them, but it was Allah who
> killed them. And you threw not, O Muhammad,
> when you threw, but it was Allah who threw that
> He might test the believers with a good test.
> Indeed, Allah is Hearing and Knowing.[87]

This "testing the believers" makes historical time and human beings' actions into figurative emanations of God's will. Thus, a mere literal interpretation is limited and compromised. To insist on literal contradictions is to blind would-be believers of the vision of the full expression of God's will. Another crucial use of such interpretation of the sacred text is presented to the followers of Muhammad:

Indeed, those who pledge allegiance to you, O Muhammad, they are actually pledging allegiance to Allah. The hand of Allah is over their hands.[88]

Then, the historical Muhammad becomes the figurative representative of God in historical time. That is, he becomes God, or the only way God can be understood in historical time. The bonded hands of believers as they pledge allegiance become the

---

[87] Sura 8:17.
[88] Sura 48:10.

representatives of God's will. This appearance of God's presence in historical time can only occur through the actions of humans, and their fate as experienced in the world. Yet, this is only a partial understating of both the wholeness of God or the Godhead and of the world to come. To interpret such actions literally, merely through a historical lens, is to be trapped in limited understanding.

Science

If science is reduced to the "I'll tell you as if you were a third grader mode" when approaching the frontiers of the temporal world we know, it is no surprise that it has left the crossing of that frontier to the prophecies and revelations that seemed rooted in a world unbound from nature. Whatever major research projects have been conducted or are envisioned by thanatology researchers—those studying death and dying—such work is no more advanced than astronomy before Copernicus.

Scientific researches suggest that after we die our consciousness goes somewhere in existence and based on some religious interpretation of death and afterlife, this is thought to be spiritual existence. Scientists tried to interpret this spiritual existence and capture any scientific evidence for what we call "the soul" however, all their attempts have failed. Eventually, with the help of the message and the knowledge of all ancient texts, it became so obvious that I have arrived at a new understanding and interpretation of death and the afterlife. It became clear that our consciousness does not exist in a spiritual realm, rather, it travels thousands or millions of years in future, until it reaches a new physical existence. It reaches what sacred texts have called "the Day of Judgment."

No doubt, deathbed studies discussed earlier show, at the moment of death, the deceased can be hyper-conscious and what is seen by them is real. This can't be explained and confirmed scientifically without a basic comprehension of the true meaning of death as experienced through revelation in the sacred texts. An expansion of consciousness leads to an awareness both unreachable and unexplainable from our temporal prisons.

Consciousness cannot be separated from the physical brain. If a dying person experiences a new type of consciousness outside of this world, that's because their newly resurrected brain is activated. Many accounts of these experiences borrow implements from our primitive cognitive toolbox, which allows us to almost fully understand those things that our senses are too dull to perceive: light in motion becomes a train, its moments of enlargement and shrinkage, the beginning and the end becoming one—altogether it is an awakening that moves beyond our understanding.

Our understanding is hobbled by the difficulty of reflecting on something that cannot be fully reflected upon. This phenomenon is nothing like watching a film montage. No matter how talented the director and editor are it is still not about enlargement or shrinkage. These are conditions only displayed by mass; ditto for any qualities of "heft," and cannot be the end and the beginning. The elements are drawn from the very primitive art of storytelling that, in the eternal present, becomes redundant.

Consciousness, as such, can be seen as continuous. We can't separate ourselves from our own consciousness. Our consciousness exists for us as a recognizable entity from the day we were in the womb till the day we die. Therefore, it seems to be constant but in actuality, it is discontinuous and malleable. At the moment of death, two types of events seem to meld and two consciousnesses are mixed. New things appear in the brain of the almost-deceased: the consciousness is here in this world, yet, it is also one step into the new physical world. At that moment saying RIP (raise in peace), will be more reasonable than saying RIP (rest in peace).

Conclusion

It seems to me, all sacred texts are connected, and if we lose one of them, we will not be able to comprehend the true meaning of death. Therefore, all narratives from these sources emanate from the same source and empty into the same ocean. The Quran, the Bible, and other ancient books lead to the revelation of a new physical life in an existence that starts at the moment of death. It can only be understood through nearness, as exerted and practiced with faith that need not be proven. We understand it through a mystery that only the ignorant might seek to penetrate and decipher.

The sacred texts tackled these issues. Some anthropologists believe a crucial development in the expansion of human consciousness and the creation of civilization itself, perhaps the last great revelation before the resurrection, and the Last Judgment, occurred when our proto-ancestors learned to concoct, reflect on, and communicate to others, the mysteries and narratives of what did not exist.[89]

Our proto-ancestors, like the angel of history, with its back to both the future and the paradise it does not remember coming from, dared cast a glance into the darkness of the unimaginable, the impossible, and realities that would never exist. Such realms became seemingly infinite and unlocked from the time past. The angel—our proto-ancestor, dared a glance at God. It lent consciousness a mystery almost as powerful as those greater mysteries it sought to decipher.

This ability, which anthropologists call "fictive thinking," may at first seem to have been a drawback to a group of creatures that faced real dangers and threats almost every single hour of their existence.[90] The ability to create a common myth, through the invention of stories and legends, allowed collective unity that set the foundation for the first complex societies. No one knows what gave

---

[89] C. Jason Throop and Charles D. Laughlin. 2007. "Anthropology of Consciousness." In *The Cambridge Handbook of Consciousness*, edited by Philip David Zelazo, Morris Moscovitch, and Evan Thompson (Cambridge: Cambridge University Press).
[90] Benjamin Y. Hayden, John M. Pearson, and Michael L. Platt. 2011. "Fictive Reward Signals in Anterior Cingulate Cortex." *Science* 324 (5929): 948–950.

rise to the instinct for such a mental switch, but the instinct remained in human beings as they confronted the mystery of death and dwelled on an existence beyond their mortal lives.

The revelation of the source of this urge toward the impossible is the moment, the experience, or the communion with God the creator, who re-creates human beings. Therefore, I have noted the veins of truth running through all prophets and their books. And if so, it becomes very hard to ignore their message. I am forced to accept the coming resurrection as a solid scientific hypothesis. If I consider the words of the prophets to be true, then I absorb the meaning of the coming Day of Judgment, which is led by a personal God or creature. I will go through this understanding in the next chapter.

Granting such paramount importance to sacred texts—and connecting the use of "fictive" language, both to the mythmaking at the heart of the creation of these texts and the development of human consciousness—helps us move on to a more sublime understanding of spiritual revelation. This understanding becomes a dual revelation because it allows human consciousness to expand beyond its fountainhead and proceed to its destined wholeness.

This perspective also brings with it its own set of complications, given the vastness of material covered in the sacred texts, and their tendency to sprout contradictions from verse to verse and waffle on "versions" of the truth. When taken out of context, the sources of sacred texts may seem less than divine, as if the Godhead were a duplicitous politician. So, context and manners of reading are important here. The contradictions cannot be addressed on a literal level because they defeat the very purpose and intent of the texts.

Chapter 9

Revelation Redux

The metaphorical model the Holy Quran employs to convey its meaning is useful to our argument. It allows us to reinterpret the verses related to Jesus's story including his death, by the will of God, who then took him to the kingdom of heaven. That is how God raised him to himself, through death that, in fact, changes our understanding of the actual historical meaning of death. The act solves the apparent contradictions in the verses when interpreted through a limited, literal perspective.

In this chapter, I will pursue the last section of the argument as a believer. I will elaborate on my understanding of life, death, and the Day of Judgment by attempting to move beyond the proof of the literal that has failed to build greater understanding. To say I now approach our topic at the end, as a believer, is not to abandon the three-pronged approach this book is founded on. My final approach helps to understand how the streams of history, morality, and faith must converge if we are to arrive at a more in-depth and sublime understanding of revelation, death, and the afterlife.

Heaven and the Future

When we hear the word "heaven," it comes to mind as a place in the sky. Actually, there is no heaven in the sky, not if the sky is understood from a scientific perspective. Science must deal with what exists and what can be proven through evidence. It can ascertain and guess at what else exists, based on proof, but it has no use for the fictive language of myth and sacred texts, nor for conceptions of what does not exist outside the realm of historical time. Science may willingly revise its conception of time, its expanse, and effects, as it often has, but it is always contained within it.

In the popular imagination, heaven may be conceived of as a place in time, especially in the future. But, through the figurative interpretation of verses such as the ones shared, we may better phrase it in the language of belief. Let's say, if heaven exists beyond the concepts of time and the future. Thus, Benjamin's angel of history must have his back turned to forces that, though they may soon be all-consuming, he cannot fully understand. That is, he cannot turn to them; it is against the baser instincts of his nature, which is trapped in historical time.

When the ancient books focus on people going to heaven after death, they talk about a place beyond themselves. In ancient times, people would have had difficulties understanding this concept. Therefore, they imagined heaven to be a place in the sky - This is not totally a misconception because, at the end of time, the earth will not be in the same place it is now.

We can consider the earth's movement in the sky as a movement toward another world, but only if we do so figuratively.

We can only achieve this with the language of myth and belief, through which the conception of time and place are arrived at through another understanding of existence.

Thus, historical time, for a believer, is seen as the process through which God expresses himself in the world through the actions of humans and all their lesser creatures. Even human beings' greatest accomplishments—those that still exist and those that have perished in oblivion, the great turmoil Benjamin's angel of history witnesses—are seen as a harvest of God's will for what is to come beyond time: "That is from the news of the cities, which we relate to you; of them, some are [still] standing and some are [as] a harvest."[91]

Such a conception, of time as a harvest, is essential to the believer's understanding of the Last Day and human beings' new consciousness in the fullness of the Godhead. In such a harvest, human consciousness is forged through deeds and misdeeds that express God's decree in this world. To claim this consciousness will be transformed in the afterlife into some nebulous force, is to negate the presence of God. Thus, for a believer, the history that delineates an individual's actions, and the morality that measures the value and worth of those actions, cannot be dismissed as the detritus of a fallen realm. They are the fundamental elements of the revelation and resurrection that is the fulfillment of God's decree.

---

[91] Sura 11:100.

The Builder and the Destroyer

If a landowner wants to build a castle, he hires builders and oversees the construction. A variety of workers build the foundation, the first floor, second, the gates, and so forth. Others, however, add new technologies, even after the castle has long been built. They improve upon it. Every worker contributes as they are best able. No worker can do all things alone.

This continues through the compounded contributions of each worker until the castle is completed. The process becomes almost organic. Others naturally replace a few workers and the very act of building becomes the raison d'etre for the community of workers. Those who do not participate are excluded from the quintessence of the whole, the full expression of the Creator's will that will culminate on the Day of Judgment. Whoever tries to stop the building or destroys it will be removed by the owner and replaced. When the castle is completed, the owner invites all those who participated in building the castle to live in it, not only as equals, but as creators of their existence.

This is a metaphor for life and the afterlife, using the power of fictive language to understand what is commonly beyond our understanding. For the owner to dismiss all the workers at the end to some desolate nowhere-land and instead invite a horde of dinosaurs to dwell in the castle, would devalue and doom the castle to destruction. It would also defeat the purpose of building it, and cast doubts on the sanity of its owner, as the person who builds castles only to condemn them to ruins. Such is the absurdity of not believing in the resurrection of human beings.

In the scriptures, it was written that at the beginning God said, "Let there be light," 92 and somehow light came to existence; God made man and woman93, identically, God said, "let there be heaven," and heaven will be, by the action of his creations by spreading truth, justice, righteousness, and peace, and by sharing and supporting each other to make the earth and sky a better place. God gave humans the ability to take advantage of everything on earth and in the sky. To test everyone, as God tests believers through their faith in his representative in historical time, God created life and death. God made it so everyone would have limited time and be brought to our world at a certain point.

This is a preparation for what is to come, of which human beings only have a skewed and limited understanding. This brings to mind the passage shared from the Holy Quran, in which Jesus's disciples are "deceived" into believing a certain interpretation about his death when God takes the prophet as his own. It may be said that they are only so deceived because of their literal understanding of events through their limited perspective. Human beings as such, trapped in nature and historical time, are deluded in their

---

[92] Genesis 1:3.
[93] Genesis 1:27–29.

understanding of the fullness of God's will as it works through them.

God is hidden in historical time because He must be, through the very nature of historical time, which cannot even begin to encompass His fullness, but only suggests it through the actions of human beings. God stands behind Benjamin's angel of history and His force is felt as it pulls the angel away from His vision of the time of man. The angel is not punished because of his obsession with historical time, but he must be pulled away by the storm behind if he is ever to experience revelation. In a human's life, the force perennially pulling them from behind is death. Revelation is only available to those willing to experience death.

The messengers and prophets interpret God's signs and allow others to see and believe. There are also those who reject the words and visions of these prophets and remain half-blind, with glances cast only on the time of human beings. God saw that there were people who would submit to His words, as they would believe in the incremental progress of righteousness, justice, and peace, so that, at the end of time, the fullness of heaven would be created. The history of human beings, and the full deployment of their moral instincts, are the foundations of this heaven.

God would not forget the people who sacrificed to survive and build the heaven, even if only with a tiny effort. Since the time of the first human, whosoever believed and walked on their beliefs would be taken to share and experience the only result of their work,

God's work, in the only language through which humans can understand their existence beyond themselves. No matter how small the amount of good deeds, what religion they followed, or whether they imagined God as a father, mother, or even as one of God's creations, because of their limited mind-set, while the most honorable description will be, "There is nothing like unto God."[94] The one who believes in the afterlife and did whatever he or she could to make the heaven, that is the culmination of human beings' time that would be a part of it, and God would reward their deeds.

On the other hand, Satan, or the representation of evil actions, challenges God so that his creation will not be able to fulfill his words and will be drowned with the sinking boat (the universe). Satan's will is to lead the creation astray from what is truthful. To accomplish his mission, Satan spreads hatred, envy, deception, and doubt to destroy peace and goodness. Some people listen and they do evil works. They are not aware however that these timely destructive actions will not change God's will. Whosoever was unwell to submit would be a part of hell and perish. Hell, in such an understanding, is the only result available in the absence of heaven, the absence of the fullness of God's will.

At the end of time, people will be judged, as they were the chosen ones, the chosen builders. Their deeds will be weighed: how much one's life has affected the past, as well as the future; how

---

[94] Sura 42:11

much it has shaped the existence beyond time; who helped in making the heaven and those who were hell-bent on destroying it. Time will end, the universe will collapse and perish, and heaven will be the Ark of life.

The Laboratory

If heaven is a place from the future, then where will it take place in this empty universe? Where life, as we know it, exists only in our planet (earth), and we do not know if life exists elsewhere in this huge universe.

To understand the position of the earth compared to the world to come (heaven), is like comparing an experimental object to factory production or comparing a tree with wide land that is ready to grow up new trees. In that sense, the earth is our laboratory, our experimental environment, or our tree that has been filled up with all kinds of fruits. These fruits are the metaphorical description of the energy resources in this earth, whether it is the food we eat or the wood we fire up.

To be unattached from these earthly fruits is the first step of enlightened in our journey to heaven; to consider these earthly fruits to be the goal is like being trapped in our laboratory, and not being able to see beyond our earthly perspective. What we consider treasures are so little compared with what will come, and what we are fighting for will be laughable when we unlock the treasures of the universe, and we reach our resurrection.

To have that honor of unlocking the treasures of the universe, to be the executors of what has been initiated, and to be what we can call "the chosen ones," we must have the belief and precognition of our goal.

The Good Life and Beyond

Heaven is the result of human actions and deeds. For every cause, there is an effect, and the last result is the tree of heaven. At this juncture, humans will be resurrected. They will find out how much their actions have affected the building, or destroying, of heaven. Even if a human being builds in the wrong direction, he will have a chance at redemption, by fixing his errors through his actions in historical time:

> Another parable put He forth before them, saying, "The Kingdom of Heaven is like a grain of mustard seed, which a man took and sowed in his field, which indeed is the least of all seeds; but when it is grown it is the greatest among herbs and becometh a tree, so that the birds of the air come and lodge in the branches thereof.[95]

As we have seen before, since sacred texts use fictive language to allow believers to conceive a world beyond their understanding, this parable cannot be taken literally through the

---

[95] Matthew 13:31–32.

process of nature. It speaks to the power that is in human beings to express God's will, and for which nature is but a stained mirror—an important tool, nonetheless. It is the only perspective that human beings have in historical time. But if they use it to understand what is beyond them, then it can become a mode of dual revelation. Human beings' actions, however, can also be mirrored in the mutations of nature, which must perish in order for the new world to arise:

> Even so, every good tree bringeth forth good fruit,
> but a corrupt tree bringeth forth evil fruit. A good
> tree cannot bring forth evil fruit, neither can a
> corrupt tree bring forth good fruit. Every tree that
> bringeth not forth good fruit is hewn down and
> cast into the fire. Therefore, by their fruits ye shall
> know them.[96]

Understood through our previous metaphor of the building of the castle, these mutations are expressive of the destructive instinct of human beings through their misled actions in historical time. It is the catastrophe that Benjamin's angel of history witnesses, and that they must be pulled away from the forces blowing at their back. The distinctions between the destroyers and the builders come from actions in historical time, the only way human beings have to

---

[96] Matthew 7:11–13.

express God's will during their time in history. Thus, it is not about false expressions of belief and worship through empty actions and gestures of belief, but of full expressions of belief through their deeds, the expression of God's will in this world. As stated in the Holy Quran:

> You see them bowing and prostrating [in prayer],
> seeking bounty from Allah and His pleasure. Their
> mark is on their faces from the trace of prostration.
> That is their description in the Torah. And their
> description in the Gospel is as a plant which
> produces its offshoots and strengthens them, so
> they grow firm and stand upon their stalks,
> delighting the sowers—so that Allah may enrage
> by them the disbelievers. Allah has promised those
> who believe and do righteous deeds among them
> forgiveness and a great reward.[97]

Even if we try to destroy or cover the seeds so they don't grow, human beings' actions will culminate in the collective fruits that become the bounty of their labors. They will become the builders of heaven and will return through their creation, which is their expression of Godly will. This is God, as incarnated in historical time, through the actions and deeds of his creation:

---

[97] Sura 48:29.

They said, "O woe to us! Indeed, we were
wrongdoers." And that declaration of theirs did
not cease until we made them [as] a harvest,
extinguished [like a fire].[98]

Ammit, Yama, Sheol, or Hell is the inevitable end of life, a
place of an endless pain, and an endless sorrow, a place of no hope,
a place of thirst, and hunger. It is a place where the destructive
forces will never have rest, and once the universe comes to an end,
whoever has not submitted to heaven, and to the ark of survival, is a
part of destruction and must perish. Heaven, while being an
expression and a culmination of human beings' actions, also
becomes the full expression of God's will through his creation. Yet,
even the attempts to thwart that will in the creation are addressed in
the holy texts and must be understood as part of the full picture:

He answered and said unto them, "He that soweth
the good seed is the Son of Man. The field is the
world, the good seed are the children of the
Kingdom, but the tares are the children of the
wicked one. The enemy that sowed them is the
devil, the harvest is the end of the world, and the
reapers are the angels. As therefore the tares are
gathered and burned in the fire, so shall it be at the

---

[98] Sura 21:14–15.

end of this world. The Son of Man shall send forth
His angels, and they shall gather out of His
Kingdom all things that offend and them that do
iniquity and shall cast them into a furnace of fire:
there shall be wailing and gnashing of teeth. Then
shall the righteous shine forth as the sun in the
Kingdom of their Father. Who hath ears to hear,
let him hear.[99]

Here I am not trying to convince anyone to believe. I'm not
inspiriting a religious system. I'm stating that only if we submit to
this understanding and vision offered by the sacred texts will we
understand their truths. Then, we are already believers. A believer
cannot be convinced, the way a scientist can, of a new interpretation
of the universe through the presentation of evidence. Such
literalness, in fact, is antithetical to the very nature of belief and its
expressive tool, the fictive language of myth. In this text, I have not
revealed a new revelation or information, rather, I have cleansed the
interpretation of the sacred texts from the impurities that were
blocking our understanding. This interpretation of human beings'
actions in historical time is never recent, it is an ancient knowledge
that was overlooked, absent or forgotten.

The crucifixion of Jesus will not be wasted. All of human
beings' good and righteous works will not be wasted. We must

---

[99] Matthew 13:37–43.

exercise patience and openness to the unknowable, through our limited perspective.

If we don't see some of the results of our good actions in this life, it has been told that, at the moment of death, we will see the future results of our works, and we will see heaven. To expect a *quid pro quo* for every good deed in historical time, is to remain trapped in ignorance about the unknowable. This way of thinking closes off the spirit from the expression of God's will. If we "disbelieve" and ignore, can't stop doing harm and destruction, or perceiving the result of our actions, then it has been told that heaven is in the process of being built by these actions. We come to know the unknowable and what is beyond us only through certain actions. We may miss the chance to experience heaven if we don't participate.

If we don't submit in building the ark, we are on our way to sink when the greatest flood comes. Maybe we think we are building something great in this life but, if it's against sharing, righteousness, justice, and peace, it will be destroyed. It doesn't matter if this evil action is requested by Satan himself or by a someone you think is God; submitting to righteousness is the right path, and we all should submit to it before it's too late, even if it's on the last day of our life. Otherwise, at the moment of death, we will face the future results of our actions. We will experience the darkness of Sheol.

It is wise to remember that such an understanding of our actions during our time in this world is skewed if we only understand the mustard seed to be a thing of science and of this world, rather than the seed of a future world. We may spend years, or our whole life chasing a belief, trying to gain a prize, build our dream house, or build a successful business—which are all great things to do, but they are temporal, and ultimately, they will be lost and vanished once we die. What will remain for us is what we will inherit from our actions in the last days, what will remain is what we have given for our future, not what we have taken from this life. The greater we give, the greater our building will be.

Resurrection and reincarnation

As a result of the scientific studies I mentioned previously in Chapters 4 and 5, and the historical knowledge I discussed in Chapters 3, 6, 7 and 8, the immediate physical resurrection at the moment of death, in my opinion is a very solid scientific hypothesis, and it may lead to a scientific theory one day in future. The interpretation of the afterlife and the understanding of heaven and hell that I discussed earlier in this chapter, is the most comprehensive and rational version of what will come after death. It is the best interpretation that aligns with our intellect and the sacred texts.

An alternative version to my argument is the concept of reincarnation, which I have highlighted in Chapter 3 as one of the prominent religious beliefs. I will not go through the injustice and harmful side of the concept of reincarnation, rather, I will compare it against the sacred texts and scientific studies.

Reincarnation is a very similar concept to my argument because it combines the moment of death with an immediate physical existence. At the same time, the living is dying and reborn again as a new being. However, it is different than my argument in another aspect. The consciousness of the new being is detached and separated from the deceased consciousness. There is no relationship between the newly born and the dying person. The new beings will not remember nor can they prove anything about their previous life. Therefore, it is as if that previous life never existed, neither will the next life exist; it is exactly as though we believe in nothingness after death. This is where reincarnation contradicts with most sacred texts, which describe death as a continuation of consciousness and an awareness of guilt and righteousness.

From a scientific perspective and based on the studies I have mentioned previously in Chapter 4 and 5, reincarnation is not an acceptable concept. It does not interpret the brain activities that occur just before death. Believers in reincarnation claim, that the new life starts at the womb of the new mother. However, the human brain in the womb is not fully developed, it cannot produce any kind of consciousness. Therefore, it cannot reflect any conscious activities in the deceased brain.

Some people on their deathbed – in uncontrolled environment- regardless of religious background, describe deathbed visions in their last moments of life to be a pleasant scene where they can see their relatives, beautiful beings, beautiful buildings, or sometimes a terrible scene of fire and terrifying beings. They never describe a womb or a hospital. The only evidence, believers of reincarnation use to prove their argument is testimonies from people, most likely children, who claim to remember their previous lives. They use a child's imagination as an evidence; nevertheless, a night dream is a previous life for a child.

Scientifically we can't separate the consciousness from the physical brain -if we assume any kind of separation, certainty, we will impact medical and science credibility. If believers in reincarnation add a new stage to the process, where the deceased consciousness will go to a spiritual stage before they enter new wombs. That stage alone demolishes their argument.

> "Just as the embodied soul continuously passes
> from childhood to youth to old age, similarly, at
> the time of death, the soul passes into another
> body. The wise are not deluded by this."[100]

This is the true meaning of reincarnation, which all of us have experienced and remembered. Our consciousness evolves every moment. It travels toward a higher being, by our righteous deeds, or toward a lower being, by our evil deeds. From childhood to youth, to old age, then by the phenomena of death, our

---

[100] Bhagavad Gita 2:13

consciousness will evolve to our resurrected body -where consciousness never discontinued.

If we can't accommodate with this assumption and belief of afterlife (judgment, heaven, and hell), we should at least provide an alternative convincing interpretation of the afterlife. We should be prepared for what will happen at the moment of our death, prepare ourselves with an intellectual concept supported by historical evidences. However, if we are not yet convinced of this meaning of death (death is an immediate transition to a future physical existence) entirely, then we are destroying the credibility of the sacred texts, we are tearing up what has been left from the holiness of the ancient books, we are burning the meaning of Christ's crucifixion, we are ignoring science, ignoring our own existence, ignoring reality, and despite all that, we are ignoring our sense of hope toward a better future.

It doesn't matter what religion we practice, or if we practice none. It doesn't matter if we don't believe in God, Jesus, or any of the prophets; if we are building and believing in a better future, we are building heaven. When we are submitting to heaven, we are under the guideline of the true -God. We should not feel bad about that, because under this guideline we will reach our ultimate goal. By submitting to this guideline, we are not doing a favor to God, we are doing a favor to ourselves.

Should we live for our present moment not worrying about the future?

The temptation of our temporal desires will trap us in a moment. What we emotionally believe to be the most joyful or the most painful, is nothing but a glance. We are distracted from what is hidden beyond the moment; what we consciously think is real, is just a shadow, a reflection of the reality we haven't yet reached. This reality is the force that holds our existence. She is pulling us toward herself, without letting go, if she does, the whole existence will collapse. She wants to make sure we have reached our resurrection, and we have built our ark, so when she lets it go, some will be left, and some will be taken. At that time, we will live our most painful or most joyful destiny.

As long as existence is changing from one state to another, we will not be able to know the reality of existence. When time ends, we will witness the birth of reality. Then we will see the real shape and form of existence, a new experience that is beyond time, beyond the natural world, beyond our language.

Eternity

"An eye for an eye, or a tooth for a tooth"[101] —if we consider this justice. Is it fair that we will be sentenced to eternity in hell for our temporal sins? Before I discuss this question, I wonder how come we never asked the same question for rewards? Is it

---

[101] Rev. Claude Hermann Walter Johns. (1904). Babylonian and Assyrian Laws, Contracts and Letters. New York: Charles Scribner's Sons. Chapter: II: THE CODE OF HAMMURABI; Exodus 21:24; Deuteronomy 19:21; Matthew 5:38; Sura 5:45.

justice to be awarded the eternity in heaven for our temporal good actions?

By the previous understanding and interpretation of heaven and hell, the dilemma of the injustice of eternity will be resolved. We are carrying on our shoulders millions of years of existence, if we decide to put it down or reject those inheritances, then we are damaging not only our own existence but also millions of years of existence. The experiences we have received were carried and evolved since the beginning of time until it reached us. It is not a recent nascent. It is an ancient evolution, that we are responsible to carry on.

The result of our temporal existence will have an impact on future existence. How we will hand it over to the next generations will determine how much we have progressed. This effect of our temporal actions has infinite reactions in the past as well as the future; in other words, the whole existence has reacted to create our intentions, actions, and the impacts of our actions. We are not alive since the beginning of time; however, the echo of our lives is heard from all existence. In this manner, our temporal life is eternal, not as living beings, but as influencers. To be condemned with eternity is absolutely the evenest judgment for our actions.

It is a struggle between destruction and salvation and a struggle between infinite possibilities as a result of our decisions and actions. All these possibilities will face an inevitable ending and will be poured into the fire and only one ending will take us to salvation.

Sometimes sacrifices shall happen to correct our way, and some people will take the hardest decisions for the sake of salvation. Jesus put himself on the cross to purify our destructive actions -sins. Without the well and guidance for that event to happen, we would not be able to reach our salvation, and definitely, we will reach other destructive possibilities.

> Jesus said to them, "Have you never read in the Scriptures:
>
> "'The stone that the builders rejected has become the cornerstone; this was the Lord's doing, and it is marvelous in our eyes'? Therefore, I tell you, the kingdom of God will be taken away from you and given to a people producing its fruits. And the one who falls on this stone will be broken to pieces; and when it falls on anyone, it will crush him."[102]

---

[102] Matthew 21:42–44

Chapter 10

Knowing God

After reaching this understanding of life and death by ancient texts, it became clear that prophets and enlightened people had a message. The question of *who is God?* was not the main topic of their message. They were forced to bring up the discussion of God when their message was rejected, and after they were accused of lying or madness. Their main message was to bring righteousness, justice, and peace to the world, which will lead to a higher existence (heaven). However, if they have been asked, *who told you about the afterlife?* or, *who will bring us back again?* They will reply "God."

People from different religions have debated for centuries the subject of *who is God?* Or *who is the true God?* or sometimes *What does God want?* Which is another important question. *How should we pray to her or him?* is yet another question. The list goes on for an infinite number of arguments, which is totally fine. The problem arises when we start to turn these debates into bloody debates and accuse one another of infidelity and hypocrisy. Instead of fighting for a better life and building heaven, we are fighting to defend our personal perspectives and imaginations of the true God or what we think God wants, forgetting the main purpose. By falling into these traps, we take faith out of its context.

The main purpose of faith is not to teach us about God; rather, it is to teach us about the afterlife, and to understand the cumulation of our actions in the next life. As believers, the only thing we have to do, is to believe in this meaning of life and death, which our intellect is able to understand and comprehend. However, understanding God is very deep and complex. The questions of *who is God? Or how God should be?* -these complex questions- are the motivations that encourage us to seek toward the unknowable, toward the secret of the whole existence.

Claiming some ancient texts teach violence and injustice can be true. This happens only if we isolate religions' legislations and laws from historical, sociological, political, cultural, and most importantly, linguistic studies. It is very ignorant if we embrace such a conclusion without studying these dimensions.

I was not planning to bring this argument into this book, but it is somehow relevant to death and the afterlife. I will not be able to fulfill the argument here, however, to elaborate, I will explain it by using an example.

Recently, Islam has been widely accused of teaching violence and to be the reference of most of the terrorist movements in the world. One of the Islamic legislations that is used to prove this accusation is killing the apostate (the one who leaves Islam), or fighting non-Muslims. At first glance, this seems to be brutal and violent, however, a deeper look will clarify our view.

It is indeed brutal and violent to fight and kill people only because they disagree with your belief, but is that what really happened? Did the prophet Muhammad fight and kill people for their disagreement?

The Quran to be the source of Islamic laws and legislations, does not give a clear direction regarding fighting non-Muslims. Scholars were inspired by Quran and Islamic history to develop what so-called "Sharia Law." To analyze and study the context of these laws, I prefer to use the source (Quran), in light of my understanding of life, death, and the afterlife.

The literal meaning of Islam is "submission" or "surrender"—it is the submission to righteousness, truth, peace, and justice which are considered to be Godly characteristics. A person considered to be a Muslim when he or she submits to these principles, and he or she becomes a builder of heaven. On the other hand, what the Quran calls "Kafir" is interpreted and translated to "disbeliever." While the word "Kafir" literally means "the one who covers" or "the one who hides." Moreover, The Arabic verb "Kfr" has almost the same meaning of the English verb "Cover."[103] Even if we consider a "disbeliever" to be the right translation to the word "Kafir," based on the Quranic context, it is irrelevant to disbelieving

---

[103] ABDULLAH AL ANDALUSI. (2016, May 5). What is a Kafir? The Confusion in English Regarding the Quranic Use of the Word 'Kafir'. Retrieved from ABDULLAHALANDALUSI.com.

in God; it actually means to disbelieve in righteousness and better life.

At the time of the prophet, leaving Islam was not a disagreement based on faith or politics. It was declaring a war against a better life, and righteousness. It was the act of covering and destroying the well of God, heaven. Not accepting Islam was rejecting and refusing any form of justice, righteousness, and peace. People who refused Islam were not debating the existence of God, instead, they were debating the purpose of a better life and righteousness. They were fighting against any law that would make them accountable for their evil actions, especially those from which they could not repent. In a contemporary sense, they were criminals, and fighting against them was the only way to bring peace to the world.

A faulty interpretation of the Quran, and the exploitation of some religious and political leaders to suppress their opponents, led to such legislations and laws. The grandson of the prophet Muhammad himself (Alhusayn ibn Ali) was put to death, in the time of the second *Umayyah caliph,*[104] by manipulating the revelation of his grandfather. In like manner, Jesus Christ was crucified by misusing the old law.

---

[104] I. K. A. Howard, Translator, The History of Al-Tabari, Volume XIX (University of Edinburg)

Shall we blame the founder of Judaism (Moses) for the crucifixion of Jesus Christ?

> "You will find others who wish to obtain security from you and [to] obtain security from their people. Every time they are returned to [the influence of] disbelief, they fall back into it. So, if they do not withdraw from you, offer you peace, or restrain their hands, then seize them and kill them wherever you overtake them. And those— We have made for you against them a clear authorization."[105]

In this verse, a disbeliever is refusing to restrain their hands, and rejecting any common law to live in peace. They are in a state of war. The verse which precedes elaborates the meaning "…So if they remove themselves from you and do not fight you and offer you peace, then Allah has not made for you a cause [for fighting] against them."[106]

The cause of fighting is not to create a believing world, however, it is to create a peaceful world. I wonder if the same situation occurs in our time, if a group of people who are terrorists - we may call them disbelievers- refuse to live by international laws, then what will be the reaction of our civilized world?

---

[105] Sura 4:91
[106] Sura 4:90

"They wish you would disbelieve as they
disbelieved so you would be alike. So, do not take
from among them allies until they emigrate for the
cause of Allah. But if they turn away, then seize
them and kill them wherever you find them and
take not from among them any ally or helper."[107]

Again, in this verse, if we interpret a disbeliever as someone who doesn't believe in the existence of God or have a personal view of God, then the claim that the Quran encourages violence would be true. However, if we interpret a disbeliever as a criminal who refuses the offer of peace and forgiveness with no trial, by migrating to righteous life, then we may reconcile a little more with Quranic verses.

That was just one example of how language can be misused to take advantage of sacred texts. A word that we can agree upon its meaning, can be misused, and manipulated to influence violence and to tear the world apart.

With all that being said, I'm not going to ignore the big questions that I have started my search with: *Does God exist?* and *Does new meaning of death and the hypothesis of resurrection prove the existence of God?* I must admit, these are still exceedingly difficult questions to answer. They are more of philosophical and

---

[107] Sura 4:89

rational questions than scientific. However, to elaborate, I must first return to the definition of God which I have mentioned in Chapter 1.

For Christianity and other monotheistic religions, "God" means "the creator and ruler of the universe and source of all moral authority; the supreme being." In this context, I will study God in light of death and afterlife.

Creationism

Discussing the beginning of existence in Chapter 1, while neglecting the idea of an afterlife, I have concluded that both religious creationism claims and scientific theories of existence have equal weight. Now that I have come to a new understanding of the afterlife and considering there is a new physical life after death, I must reevaluate the two rivals.

If something happens once, that could be a coincidence or a chance, but if something happens twice, and with a relationship to the first time, that is something astonishing. If every deceased is resurrected again at the moment of death, and if consciousness continues and remains as one -regardless of the new physical form- that something cannot happen without a decision, without an entity that reserves all information of living beings. Creating something from nothing can be explained somehow by mathematical and physical theories. Bringing back and re-creating the same thing with its own memory, that is an act of a creator. Even if we reject the idea of a creator who started the whole existence, the resurrection will force us to bow our heads to a creator, who will be there at the time when it will occur.

Monotheism and domination

In Chapter 3 I have shown that the promise of the coming resurrection and the Day of Judgment is a very ancient promise. Resurrection and the day of Judgment have been mentioned in almost all the ancient texts. It emerged since human history was recorded, and streams through human cultures and religions, since the first human civilization. It has never been forgotten, nor lost. Now, as I came to know that there is an immediate physical life after death, and as I realized that there is a comprehensive interpretation of this coming life, hell, and heaven. With the alignment of this interpretation with all the ancient texts, how are we to understand this in relation to monotheistic ideas and the domination of one God?

If someone can keep and fulfill a promise after several days, that is a good person. If people can keep their promises for years, those are trustworthy. What about an authority that can keep its promise for thousands or millions of years? For certain, that is a dominating authority, and it never drowses.

If this promise could not be changed, nor interrupted, it simply means, there are no equal powers or authorities that can challenge the highest one. Even if there are many different Gods, the one who will accomplish the promises will be the truthful.

Taking into consideration the version of the afterlife I discussed in Chapter 9, if there are many authorities, the credibility of the judgment after the resurrection will be damaged. An evil God will have a different scale than a righteous God; however, the one who makes the sentence of award or punishment is the true God.

The resurrection and afterlife, as it is mentioned in the sacred texts, requires a creator, a trustworthy, truthful, and dominating authority that never sleeps nor dies; otherwise, it is impossible to happen.

The meaning of death, I have explained in this book, does not necessarily prove the existence of God. Nothing from our realm can prove God (the source of existence). It is an insult that we put the creator and the highest authority to our test.

Finally, understanding the meaning of death (at the moment of death the deceased will experience an immediate physical resurrection). Understanding the interpretation of the afterlife in the ancient texts will lead to a higher state of awareness, which is knowing God, knowing reality.

M. A. Quraani

Email: M.A.Quraani@outlook.com

Linked-in: M. A. Quraani

Facebook: M.A. Quraani

Twitter: M. A. Quraani (@MQuraani)

List of References

A. V. Williams Jackson. (1893). *Avesta Reader.* Stuttgart, Germany: W. Kohlhammer.

ABDULLAH AL ANDALUSI. (2016, May 5). *What is a Kafir? The Confusion in English Regarding the Quranic Use of the Word 'Kafir'.* Retrieved from ABDULLAHALANDALUSI.com.

Adam Kirsch. (2006). *"The Philosopher Stoned." The New Yorker.*

Benjamin Y. Hayden, John M. Pearson, and Michael L. Platt. (2011). *"Fictive Reward Signals in Anterior Cingulate Cortex.".*

British Museum. (2011). *Journey through the Afterlife: Ancient Egyptian Book of the Dead.*

C. G. Jung. (1953). *Collected Works* (Vol. 7). Princeton, NJ: Princeton University Press.

C. Jason Throop and Charles D. Laughlin. (2007). *"Anthropology of Consciousness." In The Cambridge Handbook of Consciousness.* (M. M. Philip David Zelazo, Ed.) Cambridge: Cambridge University Press.

C. Machado. (1999). "Consciousness as a definition of death: its appeal and complexity." . *Clinical Electroencephalography.*

G. C. Anawati. (2012). *"Isa."* In *Encyclopaedia of Islam.* (Second, Ed.) Brill Online.

Holy Bible (English Standard Version). (n.d.).

J. Gwyn Griffiths. (1960). *The Conflict of Horus and Seth.* Liverpool, England: Liverpool University Press.

Jeffrey Long. (2010). *Evidence of the Afterlife.* New York: HarperCollins.

Jimo Borjigin, UnCheol Lee, Tiecheng Liu, Dinesh Pal, Sean Huff, Daniel Klarr, Jennifer Sloboda, Jason Hernandez, Michael M. Wang, and George A. Mashour. (2013). "Surge of neurophysiological coherence and connectivity in the dying brain.".

John Dominic Crossan. (2009). *Jesus: A Revolutionary Biography.* New York: HarperOne.

John H. C. Pippy. (2011). *Egyptian Origin of the Book of Revelation.* Raleigh, NC: Lulu Enterprises, Inc.

Keats, J. (n.d.). *"On Death.".*

Kevin Nelson, Peter Fenwick, Sam Parnia, and Mary Neal. (2013, December 11). Experiencing Death: An Insider's Perspective. *panel presentation, New York Academy of Sciences.*

L. T. Zagzebski. (1991). *The Dilemma of Freedom and Foreknowledge.* New York: Oxford University Press.

Mahabharata. Bhagavad Gita. (n.d.).

Mary C. Neal. (2001). *To Heaven and Back.* Colorado Springs, CO: WaterBrook Press.

Pin van Lommel. (2010). *Consciousness Beyond Life: The Science of the Near-Death Experience.* New York: HarperCollins.

Proclus. (n.d.). *Chrestomathia ii.*

Rev. Claude Hermann Walter Johns. (1904). *Babylonian and Assyrian Laws, Contracts and Letters.* New York: Charles Scribner's Sons.

Saheeh International. (2004). *The Quran English Meaning.* 1997AL-MUNTADA AL-ISLAMI: ABUL-QASIM PUBLISHING HOUSE.

Sam Parnia. (2013). *Erasing Death.* New York: HarperCollins.

Second (Ed.). (1895). *The Zend-Avesta.* (J. Darmesteter, Trans.) Oxford, England: Clarendon Press.

Sherwin B. Nuland. (1994). *How We Die.* New York: Alfred A. Knopf.

Sigmund Freud. (1950). *Totem and Taboo.* New York: W. W. Norton and Company.F

St. Thomas Aquinas. (n.d.). *"Commentary on the Gospel of St. John.".* (J. A. Weisheipl, Trans.) Albany, NY: Magi Books, Inc.

Terry Eagleton. (2009). *"Waking the Dead." New Statesman.*

The History of Al-Tabari (Vol. XIX). (n.d.). (I. K. Howard, Trans.) University of Edinburg.

The Monotheist Group. (2008). *The Message – A Translation of the Glorious Qur'an.* Brainbow Press.

Tibetan Book of the Dead. (1975). Boston, MA: Shambhala Publications, Inc.

Walter Benjamin. (2006). *Selected Writings* (Vols. 4, 1938–1940). Cambridge, MA: Belknap Press of Harvard University Press.

Wilcox, L., & George, J. (Eds.). (1994). Buffalo, NY: Prometheus Books.

Printed in Great Britain
by Amazon